How to Drive Your Competition Crazy

Two men & a Truck
upper crust
wreck Amended

Poo ping Palaw
Rent a nerd
Fudge Factu
Cheaten Tax Service
Coffin Air Service

Ransom Air line

Amigone
Electric Fetus

Also by Guy Kawasaki

Hindsights

Selling the Dream

The Macintosh Way

Database 101

The Computer Curmudgeon

How to

Creating

Drive Your

Disruption for

Competition

Fun and Profit

Crazy

Guy Kawasaki
with Michele Moreno

HYPERION
New York

All rights reserved. No part of this book may be used or reproduced in any manner whatsoever without the written permission of the Publisher. Printed in the United States of America. For information address Hyperion, 114 Fifth Avenue, New York, New York 10011.

Excerpt from "We Will All Go Together When We Go," © 1958 by Tom Lehrer. Reprinted by permission of Tom Lehrer.

Haiku by William Warriner excerpted from *101 Corporate Haiku*, © 1994 by William Warriner. Reprinted by permission of Addison-Wesley Publishing Company, Inc.

Library of Congress Cataloging-in-Publication Data

Kawasaki, Guy, 1954–
How to drive your competition crazy : creating disruption for fun and profit / by Guy Kawasaki with Michele Moreno.
p.   cm.
Includes bibliographical references and index.
ISBN 0-7868-8163-1
1. Industrial management.   2. Technological innovations.
3. Competition.   I. Moreno, Michele.   II. Title.
HD31.K347   1995
658—dc20   95-10151
                                                                    CIP

Book design by Richard Oriolo

FIRST PAPERBACK EDITION

1   3   5   7   9   10   8   6   4   2

**To my son,
Nicodemus Mathias Kawasaki.
May he drive the competition crazier
than his dad ever did.**

. . . at last I understood that writing was this: an impulse to share with other people a feeling or truth that I myself had.

Brenda Ueland, *If You Want to Write*

Contents

Part One: Lay The Groundwork

Part Two: Do The Right Things

Contents

Part Three: Do Things Right

Part Four: Push The Envelope

Acknowledgments

A book is made better by good readers and clearer by good opponents.

Friedrich Wilhelm Nietzsche, *Miscellaneous Maxims and Opinions* (1879)

Behind every successful author stands an amazed research assistant. Michele Moreno is the amazed research assistant standing behind me. If you like the examples in the book, credit her. If you don't, blame me. In any case, she did a splendid job despite the handicap of my vague and ever-vacillating direction.

The greatest gifts an author can receive are "good readers" and "good opponents" who force him to rethink what he has written and actualize what he has not. Bill Meade is such a reader. Thank goodness he found me, because he possesses one of the finest marketing minds I have ever looted. Speaking of looting, I did a number on Raleigh Muns, because I got the answer to an exercise in this book as well as many references and confirmations. He got dim sum.

To this day, the identity of the "father of Macintosh" is a controversy. Jef Raskin started the project, and Steve Jobs finished it. In the same sense, Steve Roth came up with the idea for this book, and I finished it. Without Raskin and Roth, Macintosh and *How to Drive Your Competition Crazy* might not exist.

Julie Livingston and John "I'll do it for a Performa" Michel are like family to me. At times supportive, at times demanding, and at all times humbling, they forced me to improve the form, function, grammar, and content of this book. Also, if John and Julie are like family members, then Jon Winokur is like a coach. He helped me to keep going when I was driving myself crazy writing this book.

Behind every successful author also stands an amazed editor. Rick Kot is the amazed editor standing behind me. Without his faith, I might be self-publishing this book. Without his content editing, I might be embarrassed by it. Without his advance, I might be working for Microsoft. He deserves my thanks for acquiring this book before it was real, mid-wifing it through delivery, and breast-feeding it while it was young.

Behind Rick Kot stands David Cashion and the rest of the Hyperion team: Angela Palmisono, Simone Cooper, Lisa Kitei, David Cohen, and Richard Oriolo. I'm sure I wasn't the easiest author they've ever worked with, but I bet I was the fastest. Every author should be so lucky as to work with people as good as David, Angela, Simone, Lisa, David, and Richard.

My thanks to all the readers and information sources who gave unselfishly of their time and expertise: Richard Barlow, Louise Bates, Chris Calande, Dan and Pam Chun, Vicki Clift, Sam Decker, Howard Getson, Debra Goldentyer, Helen Gracon, John Holland, Steve Kopp, Steven Long, Terri Lonier, Bill Lutholtz, Will Mayall, Dave Millman, Wayne Muromoto, Adam Robinson, Bobbi and Peter Silten, Kenneth Sobel, Harry Somerfield, Todd Spare, Michael Stein, Anne Taylor, Richard Theriault, Stephanie Vardavas, Elizabeth Williams, and Marcia Yudkin. Special thanks also go to Susan Bright Winn, who transcribed the interviews.

Readers unaccustomed to computers may find this strange, but I want to acknowledge Dialog Information Services. This is an online information provider—enabling me to search hundreds of business and news publications without leaving my desk. A book like this could have been written without Dialog (and Raleigh Muns), but only by a masochist or an idiot.

My thanks to Pat Bechelli and the staff at Bechelli's restaurant in the Marina district of San Francisco. I spent many hours there working on this book—sometimes coming in for breakfast and staying long enough to have lunch. Some authors need scotch to write—I need the Bechelli's granola special.

Finally, I wish to thank my wife Beth for putting up with me while I wrote this book. Do you really want to know how to drive your competition crazy? Marry a terrific woman.

F o r e w o r d

E very day I get letters from people who ask how they can become a syndicated cartoonist like me. I usually tell them to forget cartooning and enter the dry cleaning profession. My logic is that I don't need more competition in cartooning, but I would like to see more competition in dry cleaning so my bills would decrease.

It's been my observation that most people are clueless, including me. You probably shouldn't assume you already understand how to be competitive. If your idea of competition is limited to stuff like pricing, channel development, and market segmentation, then you'll learn a lot by reading *How to Drive Your Competition Crazy*. I did.

After I finished reading Guy's book, I started developing plans for squashing the cartoonists who compete against me on the comics page. My plan is to define them as being bad for the environment. I've noticed that most of my competitors use a lot of ink in an attempt to be artistic.

While this is all fine and dandy from an aesthetic standpoint, I'll bet you didn't know it's destroying the rainforests.

In contrast, my comic "Dilbert" employs a planet-friendly three-panel format and an economical approach to ink usage. Moreover, I recycle many of the jokes found in "Garfield" so as not to deplete the earth's precious reserves. (In case you're wondering, I did read the part of the book about ethics. Then I read the chapter about thinking "outside the box." You might want to read those parts in the reverse order.)

For some reason, many people fail to recognize that they live in a competitive world. I'm not complaining; as long as my competitors continue to seek my advice there will be plenty of places to take my dry cleaning.

Still, I feel some social responsibility to help people become more competitive. That's why I recommend that you read *How to Drive Your Competition Crazy*. It can help you succeed in business. But, more importantly, while you're reading it, you can't practice cartooning.

Scott Adams
Author of the comic strip "Dilbert" ™

Read Me First

We must not hope to be mowers,
And to gather the ripe gold ears,
Unless we have first been sowers
And watered the furrows with tears.

It is not just as we take it,
This mystical world of ours,
Life's field will yield as we make it
A harvest of thorns or of flowers.

Johann Wolfgang von Goethe, "Perseverance"

Gotcha!

G iven the usual title of "Introduction," only a few people would read this chapter. I hope that a peculiar title like "Chapter 0" will have a profoundly different result.

This book celebrates the use of clear thinking, shrewdness, guts, and hard work to drive one's competition crazy. Here are three samples of the ideas we will examine:

✓ A pizza chain entering the Colorado market offered a two-for-one promotion to anyone who brought in the Yellow-Pages ad of its competition. It's hard to call other pizza places when their ads are gone.

✓ Fifty years ago Richard Sears made his catalog smaller than Montgomery Ward's, so that people would stack the Sears catalog on top of Montgomery Ward's. His concept was that whatever catalog was on top would be used more often.

✓ When Bank of America closed down some of the branches of Security Pacific after the two banks merged, First Interstate Bank dispatched trucks to these branches to sign up customers.

This book will help you delight your customers, increase sales and profits, and frustrate your competition. However, no book is a panacea. This book can show you *how*, but you have to *do*. After all, greatness is won, not awarded.

How This Book Is Organized

When many authors are asked, "What is your book about?" they are tempted to answer, "About twenty bucks." Jokes aside, I will explain the organization of my book to help you get as much value and enjoyment from it as possible.

How to Drive Your Competition Crazy is made up of four parts. Each part contains four chapters.

■ **Lay the Groundwork** is a concession to the left side of my brain, which tells me that people should plan, prepare, and premeditate their actions, or they might get burned to a crisp.

The first chapter of this section illustrates why driving your competition crazy is a positive force. Then, the following three chapters explain what you need to get started: a knowledge of yourself, your customer, and your enemy.

■ **Do the Right Things** reflects my belief that the key to driving your competition crazy is making the proper strategic choices. Success in business, even guerrilla business, comes from smart, careful decisions—not berserk and chaotic attacks.

The four chapters of this section explain the fundamental actions that are necessary to make customers happy—which is, ultimately, the best way to drive your competition crazy.

■ **Do Things Right** illustrates the point that, having made the necessary commitment to your customer, the Zen is in the implementation. You can know the recipe and have the ingredients, but you still have to knead the dough just so.

These four chapters describe the *hows*—that is, the processes, procedures, and practices that will please your customers and, therefore, drive your competition off the deep end.

■ **Push the Envelope** presents daring, unexpected, and bleeding-edge methods that will ruin your competition's day. It is the last section because it contains ideas that are too dangerous for amateurs, so don't try these techniques without proper supervision.

Two chapters in this section explain how to be an opportunist and an unconventional thinker. A third illustrates how to drive internal competition crazy (aka, a lousy boss). Finally, the last chapter describes a few defensive methods to keep the upper hand.

The Zen of Examples

Throughout this book I've included many examples of companies and people driving their competition crazy. Admittedly, the odds are low that these anecdotes are directly applicable to your own business, but that isn't the point.

What is the point? First, to help you understand the *principle* that each example embodies. Teaching a person how to fish is more valuable than giving him a fish. Second, to enable you to experience the wink and glee that accompany driving your competition crazy.

One more thought about examples: my book—and, in my opinion, every business book—contains examples as if the author knew the exact circumstances of their origins. We don't. Perhaps Richard Sears made his catalog smaller than Montgomery Ward's because he got a deal on smaller paper.

Biology contains the same predicament. Books tell us the giraffe's long neck is an adaptation that enables the species to eat tasty leaves on the top of acacia trees. But says who? As Harvard biology professor Stephen Jay Gould opines, "Current utility may not be equated with historical origin, or, when you demonstrate that something works well, you have not solved the problem of how, when, or why it arose."[1]

Luckily for business-book writers, business people don't really care about how, when, or why a good idea came to be—what matters is the existence of the idea and putting it to good use: "A giraffe has a long neck to eat leaves at the tops of trees? We can do that, too."

This is the Zen of examples, so read and reap.

Déjà Blue

E nough introducing. Let's get started by examining an epic battle in which I was a foot soldier. One competitor was large and the other small. One was established and the other new. One was six-colored and the other blue.

I am referring, of course, to the battle between Apple and IBM.* It is one of the best examples of David (a brave shepherd) driving Goliath (an undefeatable bully) crazy, so let us begin there.

Kawasaki

Guy Kawasaki
Cupertino, California

---

*If you've read my other books, you may be tired of my using this example. Sorry, but in order to find another one I'd have go back to working for someone else, and I'm not about to do that.

P.S.: If you'd like to get in touch with me, here is how:

- 415-325-2022

- 415-325-2023 fax

- Macway@aol.com

Note

[1]Stephen Jay Gould, *Bully for Brontosaurus: Reflections in Natural History* (New York: W. W. Norton & Company, 1991), 114.

Part One

Lay the

Groundwork

If you're going to drive your competition crazy—or if you expect to even annoy it—you have to lay a firm foundation for your efforts. Part I explains how to accomplish this. The first task is to choose a worthy opponent (Chapter 1, Mighty Opposites). Then, in order to choose the right approach to getting under the skin of this foe, you need to know these things: who you are (Chapter 2, Know Thyself), who your customers are (Chapter 3, Know Thy Customer), and who your competitors are (Chapter 4, Know Thy Enemy).

Mighty Opposites

Make no little enemies—people with whom you differ for some petty, insignificant personal reason. Instead, I would urge you to cultivate "mighty opposites"— people with whom you disagree on big issues, with whom you will fight to the end over fundamental convictions. And that fight, I can assure you, will be good for you and your opponent.

Thomas Watson, Jr., founder of IBM

The Macintosh Division

Our dream was simple: send IBM back to the typewriter business holding its Selectric typewriter balls. We were members of the Macintosh Division of Apple Computer. This means we were the hand-picked soldiers of Steve Jobs, cofounder of Apple Computer.

The year was 1984. We had just shipped an insanely great computer for "the rest of us,"* and we were on a mission to destroy our mighty opposite, IBM. We had chosen this company as our mighty opposite because it believed in centralized, autocratic, and user-indifferent (at best) or user-unfriendly (at worst) computing. We believed in decentralized, democratic, and user-friendly (at least) computing.

My role in the Macintosh Division was to evangelize software companies to create Macintosh products. The introduction of a new computer requires defeating a self-fulfilling prophecy: If there's not enough software, no one will buy the computer, but if no one buys the computer, there's little reason to write software. I used fervor and zeal but never money to bestir these companies to take the leap of faith.

We worked ninety hours a week and loved it because we were on a crusade both to change the world and to prevent domination by the blue-suited meanies. Our mighty opposite aroused passions that customers could not. Though we were *excited* by the thought of pleasing customers, we were *incited* by the thought of destroying IBM's hegemony.

Working in the Macintosh Division I learned that people like to compete. It satisfies a human need for drama whether it involves pleasing people, overcoming adversity, or defeating mediocrity. That's why there are chili cook-offs, pickup basketball games, spelling bees, and beauty contests in cities and towns across America.

Creating Advantages

Succeeding against IBM required us to diminish IBM's advantages and to create new advantages for Apple. IBM's primary advantage was its legitimacy as a business-computer vendor because, as the saying went,† "No one ever got fired for buying an IBM."

By making a computer with dazzling software that was easier to use, we intended to diminish the attractiveness of buying from IBM: you might not get fired for buying an IBM, but you wouldn't get the best personal computer. Here's what we did:

---

*That is, people who refused to be lemmings and hated using existing personal computers.
†Not "goes."

- First, we created an advantage called the Macintosh user interface. This interface, based on iconic representations of real-world objects such as a trash can and file folders, "automagically" made computers easy to learn and easy to use for nontechnical people.

- Second, we fostered innovative applications like the desktop publishing program called PageMaker. Macintosh software wasn't merely rehashed versions of existing MS-DOS and Apple II products. It was next-generation software that, using the words of management gurus Paul Sherlock and Tom Peters, made people "glow" and "tingle" and scream, "Wow!"

- Third, we incited customers to evangelize Macintosh and turn it into a cause. These unpaid salespeople propped up Macintosh during the period when very little software was available and the computer was too slow—which was, trust me, a painfully long time.

Creating Disruption

As ridiculous as it now sounds, we believed we could push IBM out of the personal computer business. Obviously we failed, but we had a great time, and we did make Macintosh a success. In hindsight, we should have set a more realistic goal: to drive IBM *crazy* instead of *out of business*.

What does "driving your competition crazy" mean? It could refer to the effect Moby Dick had on Captain Ahab:

> The lightning flashes through my skull; mine eyeballs ache and ache; my whole beaten brain seems as beheaded, and rolling on some stunning ground.[1]

The imagery is scintillating, but this definition won't fly with corporate lawyers or the Federal Trade Commission. Instead, I offer a kinder, gentler definition:

> To disrupt a marketplace in order to create new advantages for yourself and to diminish the existing advantages of the competition.*

*This definition was inspired by Richard D'Aveni's book, *Hypercompetition—Managing the Dynamics of Strategic Maneuvering* (New York: The Free Press, 1994).

The anti-IBM "no blue suits" symbol used by Apple.

Ironically, the goal of this book is to help you decrease competition by achieving unfair leverage. William Kingston said it best: "... 'marketing know-how' is not knowledge of how to make a market, but how to make a monopoly."[2]

This definition implies that you don't have to destroy your competition or force it out of business—you just have to disrupt things. Apple drove IBM crazy because it succeeded in disrupting the computer industry. IBM would have been perfectly happy for the computer industry to proceed along the path of centralized and user-hostile mainframe computers.*

From IBM's perspective, kids wearing Birkenstocks and T-shirts in California created a computer that it had to acknowledge and eventually imitate because its customers demanded greater ease of use. (Surely you don't believe that IBM would have adopted graphical user interfaces like Windows or OS/2 unless it had to.) Apple didn't put IBM out of business, but it forced IBM to follow. Every dogma has its day.

---

*At one point IBM even called its personal computer division the *Entry* Systems Division. The implication was that personal computers were an entry point from which you moved when you needed a *real* computer.

How to Choose an Enemy

I t's been ten years since Apple introduced Macintosh, and I no longer work for Apple. I can now see the folly of trying to do in IBM, but I can also see the value of competing with a mighty opposite like IBM.

As Shakespeare said, "Sweet are the uses of adversity."[3] IBM forced us to create a better product. Had IBM not existed as an enemy, we would have had to find another one. Battling a company that spent more on paper clips than we did on marketing was scary, uplifting, and exciting.

Jay Levinson, the guerrilla marketing guru, validates the desirability of an adversary: "The role of your competition is to force you to get better, to keep you honest, to give validity to your industry, and to give you the resistance that you need. If you're lucky, your competitors are good, smart, and working hard—they're not just pushovers."

Good Versus Bad Enemies

The experience of working for Apple and competing against IBM taught me about the differences between a good enemy and a bad one. Apple, for example, had its pick of at least three enemies:

- Mighty-opposite IBM, the mainframe computer company that approached computing from the top down

- Upstart Compaq, a company that, like Apple, believed in the concept of personal computers but differed on user interface

- Fading Kaypro, a company whose time had come and gone

IBM was the right choice because it was the company that fundamentally opposed our vision of computing. Furthermore, it was a good enemy because a good enemy forces you to improve your company. Competing with a good enemy excites your employees and builds credibility for you in the marketplace.

Compaq was not a good enemy. Like Apple, it was a start-up, so no credibility would accrue to Apple for defeating it, and, speaking as someone who was there, we couldn't get excited about competing with Compaq. We were after bear: beating IBM and changing the world.

Kaypro was also not a good enemy. It had already begun to fade from the personal computer industry scene. Defeating it would have been meaningless. Losing to it would have been catastrophic.

Thus, I learned that a good enemy is usually an industry leader that is larger, older, and richer than your own company. A bad enemy is usually an upstart—aggressive and hungry and willing to fight viciously.

Defining a good enemy as a big, successful company and a bad enemy as a small, hungry one may seem counterintuitive. Wouldn't it make more sense to compete against a smaller company? The answer is no, and here's why:

- Trying to defeat a small company is risky. If you are successful, the victory is insignificant. If you fail, the embarrassment is huge. There's more downside than upside in this kind of contest.

- Defeating a small company may be more difficult because it may be able to mobilize quickly, change directions on short notice, and fight a guerrilla war as well as you can. Also, a small company is likely to rally more team spirit in its shipping department than a large company can in all of its facilities.

- You can define "victory" against a large enemy on your own terms. It's not necessary to put a large enemy out of business—victory can be as simple as a gain in market share. On the other hand, a true victory against a small company requires total annihilation.

True Versus False Enemies

The good-enemy relationship is usually not reciprocal. For example, IBM was a good enemy for Apple, but Apple was not a good enemy for IBM. Why? Because Apple was not the *true* enemy of IBM. The true enemy of IBM was ignorance—specifically, ignorance of the advantages of democratizing information. The company could not bring itself to consider personal computers as real computers.*

*Thus, when IBM faced many problems in the early nineties, Apple's success was only a symptom of IBM's ignorance and not a cause of IBM's difficulties.

In business you are not only free to choose between good and bad enemies but also between true and false enemies. The good-versus-bad parameter, as we've discussed, refers to the *attractiveness* of an enemy. The true-versus-false parameter refers to the *appropriateness* of an enemy.

Appropriateness has to do with whether you are fighting the right enemy—good or bad. If you're not careful, you might compete with the wrong company while your true enemy remains unidentified or unchallenged, and then you may find yourself blindsided by other organizations.

For example, Polaroid enjoyed twenty-eight years of monopoly control of the instant photography market. Then in 1976 Kodak introduced a competitive camera and film. Polaroid immediately sued Kodak for patent infringement, and it eventually won the case in 1990. The court forced Kodak to remove its camera and film from the market, and Polaroid reestablished control of the instant photography market. However, in the meantime Polaroid faced an eroding market because it had not paid attention to videocassette recorders and one-hour photo stores that had reduced the competitive advantage of instant photography.[4]

Like IBM, your true enemy may not be another company at all but internal and external factors. Internal factors include myopia, resistance to change, lethargy, confusion, and arrogance. External factors include consumer uncertainty of the benefits of your product category and people's adherence to the status quo. Apple's true and external enemy, for example, was people's ignorance of the benefits of using a graphical user interface.

We'll come back to enemies in Chapter 4. Right now it's time to lay

---

E x e r c i s e

True or False?

Woolite competes with dry cleaners.   ■ T ■ F

**United Airlines competes with
videoconferencing.**   ■ T ■ F

**Federal Express competes with
electronic mail.**   ■ T ■ F

Spouses compete with computers.   ■ T ■ F

---

the groundwork for driving your competition crazy, and the first step is to learn more about yourself.

Notes

[1] Herman Melville, *Moby-Dick* (New York: Penguin, 1992), 551.

[2] William Kingston, *The Political Economy of Innovation* (The Hague: Martinus Nijhoff, 1984), 7.

[3] *As You Like,* II.i.12.

[4] Avinash Dixit and Barry Nalebuff, *Thinking Strategically—The Competitive Edge in Business, Politics, and Everyday Life* (New York: W. W. Norton & Company, 1991), 154–55.

Chapter 2

Know Thyself

Ignorance is not bliss—it is oblivion.

Philip Wylie, *Generation of Vipers*, 1942

"You meet the nicest people on a. . . ."

C an you name the company described below?

In the fifties it had achieved great success with a line of motorcycles in Japan and started looking for new markets to conquer. In 1959
the company introduced its motorcycles in America.

At the time a "Made in Japan" label implied that a product was junk,
and the company's initial motorcycles for the American market supported

this stereotype because they leaked oil and quickly burned out their clutches.

The company's first hit in America was discovered almost by accident. The three men who spearheaded the American effort used a scooter for errands because they had only one car. This motorcycle, called the Super Cub, attracted a great deal of attention even though it had a small (fifty-cubic-centimeter) engine.

The company followed the success of the Super Cub with bigger and better motorcycles. Four years after its arrival in the United States, the company sold more than 100,000 motorcycles. This number exceeded the sales volume in America of all other motorcycle companies combined.

In 1969 the company began selling a tiny, tinny car called the N600 in Hawaii. The next year it sold the N600 in California, Oregon, and Washington. The company's distribution strategy involved asking its motorcycle dealers to get into the car business. Later this strategy changed to begging dealers of American cars to sell the N600 on the side of its showrooms.

Five years after entering the American car market with the N600, the company had sold only forty-three thousand cars in this foreign land. The next year its sales volume more than doubled. In 1976 *Motor Trend* named the company's latest model, the Accord, the "Import Car of the Year," and the company's sales started to explode in America.

In 1986 the company created a new, luxury-car marque. This product line won enthusiastic approval from the automotive press and successfully competed with BMW and Mercedes as well as American car manufacturers. In 1987 the J. D. Power Customer Satisfaction Index ranked the new marque as the best of any brand sold in America. Arguably, this company's products forced American manufacturers to remake their product lines in order to compete.

Over a twenty-year period, its strategy became clear: enter a market at the low end, achieve high volume, and then expand the product line with better and better products. Who would have predicted that the Super Cub would lead to a problem for General Motors, Ford, and BMW?

The company is, of course, Honda. The lesson here is that to drive your competition crazy, you need to understand yourself: your identity, goals, and expertise. This chapter explains how.

Define Your Company's Identity

T ake your phone off the hook, shut your door, turn off your computer, and spend the next thirty minutes thinking about three questions:

- First, what business is your company really in?

The usual tendency is to define one's business too narrowly. For example, Wang Laboratories of Lowell, Massachusetts, defined its business as making a wordprocessing computer. Had it defined its business as enhancing productivity, then it might have seen the folly of producing a computer that did only word processing. The lesson: Never confuse focus and shortsightedness.

E x e r c i s e

The Lego Company makes colorful building bricks for children. What business is Lego in?[1]

a. **Toys**

b. **Plastics**

c. **Child development**

d. **Construction**

By contrast, Honda isn't a motorcycle, car, lawn mower, or generator company although it manufactures—among other products—motorcycles, cars and lawn mowers. It is in the engine business, and its core competence is converting fuel to power.

- Second, where do you see your company in five, ten, twenty, and fifty years?

Another tendency is to define a business within too short a time frame. Honda introduced its first motorcycle to the United States in 1959.

Twenty-seven years later it introduced the Acura line of luxury cars in America. For a transition like the one from motorcycles to luxury cars, you must think in terms of long time frames.

As a contrast to Honda, consider what happened to the companies in the ice-harvesting business. From the 1830s to the 1890s ice harvesting (cutting up frozen ponds and selling the ice) was a huge industry in New England. In 1886, the biggest ice harvest that ever occurred amounted to 25 million tons.[2]

By the 1920s, almost all the ice-harvesting companies were out of business. Ice harvesting had been made obsolete by ice-making plants that could operate in any part of the country during every season. Later, these ice-making plants were themselves made obsolete with the advent of refrigerators in people's homes.

E x e r c i s e

Suppose you could go back in time and ask the owners of the ice-harvesting companies what their reactions were to ice-making machines. What do you think they would tell you?

- Third, if a prospective customer doesn't buy from you, whom does he or she buy from?

After you're done thinking about what you do and where you want to be, double-check whom the marketplace thinks is your competition. Wang Laboratories probably thought that it was competing with other word-processing companies, like NBI.* But Wang's customers probably would have told them that they were buying computers and word-processing *software*—not dedicated word processors. If Wang had known (or paid attention to) this, they might be a thriving company today.

---

*Not that this has anything to do with driving your competition crazy, but did you know that NBI stood for Nothing But Initials? NBI no longer exists. Perhaps this is because the world is not kind to companies with so little purpose that they name themselves via a joke on customers.

Exercise

Create a one-page resume for your company as if it were a person applying for a job. Include experience, education, accomplishments, and references.

Define Your Products and Services

The next step on the road to self-knowledge is to define your product or service. This exercise provides a cross-check—that is, if you're in one business but your products serve another—and it enables you to gain a true understanding of your product in order to create new markets or penetrate existing markets. For example, Honda is in the engine business, so its products convert fuel to power. But what benefit do its motorcycles provide its customers? Asked another way, what does owning a motorcycle really mean?

For many people motorcycles mean freedom and fun. It isn't a matter of personal transportation as much as personal expression. Appropriately designed and marketed, motorcycles can, therefore, attract young professionals and students who are not traditional motorcycle prospects.

Honda created a market with its motorcycles where none existed before by producing a new, hip, and user-friendly vehicle—a perfect illustration that understanding your product can enable you to see new, more effective, and perhaps unexpected ways to market it.

My buddies at Dialog Information Services, the online database company that enables people to access an ocean of information, provide an example of untapped potential. This company seems to think it is serving a small institutional market of librarians. It is underestimating its market because writers (like me) use Dialog for background research, entrepreneurs search its trademark and patent databases, and scientists access its industry journals.

Defining your product or service is a straightforward exercise, so take some time to answer these questions:

- What benefits does your product or service really provide?

- What are the most important reasons your best customers buy from you?

- How is your product positioned in the marketplace—high end, low end, price leader, etc.?

- If a prospect doesn't buy your product or service, what does he or she buy?

- Are your customers using your products in ways you never intended? Is there an opportunity there?

E x e r c i s e

Take a sheet of paper and draw a line down the middle. On the left side, write down the six most important features of your product. On the right side, for each feature, write what you'd say if a prospective customer said to you, "So what?"*

Define Your Management Style and Philosophy

The final step on the road to self-knowledge is to examine your management style and philosophy—because knowing yourself entails knowing whether you've got the right stuff to drive your competition crazy. The critical question is:

- Which of the following management styles best describes your company?

Contented Cows

Contented cows have already made it. They are often in mature industries and are living off their momentum and past accomplishments.

*Inspired by Hal Pawluk of The Pawluk Group, Inc., of Los Angeles, California.

Decision-making is usually top down and authoritarian. They are defensively oriented—trying to preserve their position, cash, and image.

Contented cows are concerned with being driven crazy—not driving other companies crazy. Thus, they are poor candidates to disrupt the marketplace—in truth, they want to preserve the status quo of the marketplace.

Leaders

Leaders have recently moved to the front of the pack in their industries because of the quality of their product, marketing, or customer service. There are usually two or three leaders in an industry. Decision-making is concentrated in middle managers. They use both defensive tactics to protect their lead and offensive tactics to lengthen it.

Leaders are positioned to drive their competition crazy because they have the requisite aggressive attitude and the resources to back it up. Leaders also make excellent "mighty opposites" because they force their competition to perform well.

Upstarts

Upstarts are the companies that are striving to join the leaders. They are active, opportunistic aggressors who fight a zero-sum game with the leaders: that is, their gain is the leaders' loss, and their loss is the leaders' gain. They often cite their enemies in their marketing plans. Decision-making is usually concentrated in a founder or a small group of employees.

Upstarts are also excellent companies to drive the competition crazy. What they lack in resources *vis-à-vis* leaders, they make up in additional aggressiveness and zeal. Disrupting the marketplace is to their advantage, because the status quo favors leaders and contented cows. They also make bad enemies because they have little to lose.

Guerrillas

Guerrillas are small, non-mainstream companies. They survive by hitting and running and appealing very strongly to a small part of the population. They are offense-minded because they have nothing to defend. Decision-making is in the trenches, and they succeed because of their perseverance.

Guerrillas know nothing except disrupting the marketplace and driving their competition crazy. They may even view driving their competition crazy as an end in itself. If guerrillas attract enough customers, they can acquire the strength to challenge upstarts, leaders, and contented cows.

E x e r c i s e

Take a piece of paper and draw a picture of your company and write a one-line caption. Have your fellow employees do this exercise. Compare your drawings.[3]

A Caveat

This discussion of management styles implies that a company adopts one style and retains that style forever. This is not the case. The contented cows of one decade may rise to the occasion and become leaders, upstarts, or guerrillas. For example, as Honda disrupted the American car business it progressed from being a guerrilla to an upstart to a leader.

However, the U.S. car manufacturers woke up toward the end of the eighties and produced better cars, and they re-disrupted the car business, competed effectively with Honda, and changed the perception that Japanese cars were great and American cars were junk.

Also, different parts of a company can exhibit radically different management styles. For example, the independent business unit charged with bringing a new discovery to market may be a guerrilla organization within a contented cow.

Get a Reality Check

Most of this chapter has involved *self*-analysis and *self*-examination. However, staring at your navel can make you hallucinate, so the final step in the process of knowing yourself is getting a reality check. Here's my four-step way to do this:

1. List the top five reasons your customers buy from you.
2. Find out who your best customers are from sales or accounting records.
3. Take the top ten customers to lunch (one at a time!) and ask them why they buy from you.
4. Compare your list and your customers' responses.

If you don't get at least one answer that surprises you from each customer, I will buy you a lunch. Also, if you can pull it off, an even more valuable process to complete is:

1. List the top five reasons potential customers don't buy from you.
2. Take ten prospective customers to lunch and ask them why they don't buy from you.
3. Compare your list and your prospective customers' responses.

If you don't get at least two answers that surprise you from each potential customer, I will buy you another lunch.

Interview: Chin-Ning Chu

From time to time, I include interviews with experts in this book. The first interviewee is Chin-Ning Chu. I've enlisted her help to explain the Zen of the process discovered in this chapter, because knowing yourself is an Eastern philosophy kind of thing.

Chin-Ning Chu was born in mainland China and emigrated to Taiwan in 1949 at the age of three, after the fall of China to the Communists. At the age of twenty-two, she left Taiwan to live in America.

Chu is a management consultant and speaker. To Asians, she is an interpreter of America. To Americans, she possesses the wisdom of the East. She has written three books about her knowledge: *The Chinese Mind Game*, *The Asian Mind Game*, and most recently, *Thick Face Black Heart: The Path to Thriving, Winning & Succeeding*. This last book established her reputation when it soared to best-seller status in several Asian countries.

Thick Face, in Chu's words, refers to a "positive self-image despite the criticism of others" that enables a person to "put self-doubt aside." Black Heart "is the ability to take action without regard to how the consequences will affect others. A Black Heart is ruthless, but it is not necessarily evil."[4]

Q: How does one get to "know thyself"?

First, you have to have a desire to know yourself. You have to have an awareness that knowing thyself is important to your mental, spiritual, and financial well-being. Then, hopefully, you have a desire to watch your every movement.

You have to be your own policeman. Why did I behave that way? Was it good or bad? You'll start to see if there's a pattern. Knowing thyself is difficult because nobody can know you better than you.

There's another way to know thyself, and that is to dive into your center. When you dive very deep into yourself, you know things naturally. For example, if I had to read a book about how to write a book, I probably couldn't finish a book. When I go to who I am, then I know how to write a book because I'm not bothered by the rules of writing books.

Q: How does this transfer to business?

People should have technical knowledge, but if they only have this, they will be dysfunctional. Most waiters see waiting on tables as delivering food. That's the technical part: take an order, deliver food to the customer, and do it well. But that's not his job. His job is to make his customer happy.*

Rules and technique are very good, but there's a point at which you have to go beyond the rules and the formulas because no matter how good you are, you are only as good as those people who set the standards for you. When you go within yourself, you're going to discover you can be better than anybody else.

*Remember the discussion of not defining your business too narrowly?

Q: What if you're a mediocre and lazy person?

Then you don't have a desire to know thyself, do you?

Q: How does your concept of "black heart" relate to knowing thyself?

"Black heart" means you're so black you can do anything—nothing is beneath you. Black heart has three stages. The first stage is winning at all costs—you even feel good about it. The second stage is that you start to feel that the fruit of success is a little bitter so you start on an inward journey.

The problem of knowing thyself is you're going to find out you don't like yourself very much. When you don't look within, you think you're so good. When you start to look within, you find knowing thyself is a very painful and courageous process. Not everyone is willing to go through it because ignorance is bliss. However, the process of knowing thyself empowers you.

The third stage is the warrior stage. In the third stage, a person sees that making a living is not separate from the sublime, spiritual state, and that the spiritual elements and day-to-day living should be integrated.

A really good businessman, scientist, artist, singer, or stonemason— a really good anything—understands this. Socrates once saw his father, a stonecutter, making a lion and asked him, "How do you do that?" His father told him, "You have to see the lion within the stone; the lion's already there; you've got to free the lion."

How do you do that? It goes beyond the technique of a stonecutter. You have to have a kind of spiritual, intuitive sense. That you get from knowing thyself. When you begin the process of knowing thyself, mysteries unfold. The more you know yourself, the more you know your world and how you fit in.

Q: How do you avoid getting stuck in the first stage?

You cannot prevent it. Somehow grace has to touch you. When you're in the dark, somebody has to lift the veil and let the light in. There is a divine intervention coming through either great things or horrible things happening to you.

These things make you start looking for answers and start looking within, so that every misfortune is an opportunity for you to start to know yourself better. Maybe it's a divine way to tell you that you're not doing things so right, so life is not going too good.

Q: It seems like much of "black heart" involves "killer instinct." How do you develop killer instinct?

Killer instinct comes from the heart's willingness to go like that [makes a slashing motion]. A surgeon takes a knife and makes the first cut. It has to be very quick, very precise, and without a shaky hand. If you give a medical student a knife, there's a little shaking in his heart. There is a training process for killer instinct.

Whenever you hesitate, you have to center yourself—go to yourself, the part that is very deep, very strong, and very still. You go to that part and execute that thing that you don't want to do. If you do that enough, you start to be in touch with that place where the effective execution exists.

Also, killer instinct has to do with keeping your eyes on the objective, because if the objective is greater than your fear or uncomfortableness, then you can break through. Killer instinct doesn't function alone. Killer instinct always has to go with the love of *dharma*, the righteousness of your cause. You have to do something that's worthwhile.

Q: What is the role of anger?

If you can provoke your enemy's emotion in a battlefield, he is going to lose his balance and his good judgment. He's going to make a wrong move. If you can provoke his sense of self-importance, he's going to do wrong things to try to prove his importance because you challenge his ego.

You can also provoke your own anger and provoke your own staff's anger to reach excellence. Anger can work destructively and constructively. Sometimes your opponent disgraces you or you fail, and this makes you so angry that anger can be the springboard into something greater.

Q: What if you provoke an enemy to excellence?

You have to know how to use strategies because every strategy can also work against you. In fact, no strategy can be the best strategy when you are trying to strategize out of fear and out of eagerness rather than total calm and total clarity.

Ultimately, you're not even competing with others. You're competing with yourself for your own excellence. If you're competing with others, maybe your target is too low. When you compete with a person, you only have to be as good or better than the person to win.

If you compete with yourself, there is no limitation to how good you can be. Also, when you compete with others, there is an end. When you compete with yourself, there is no ending until you die.

Notes

[1]Stan Rapp and Thomas Collins, *Beyond MaxiMarketing: The New Power of Caring and Daring* (New York: McGraw-Hill, Inc., 1994), 108.

[2]James M. Utterback, *Mastering the Dynamics of Innovation* (Boston: Harvard Business School Press, 1994), 146–57.

[3]Grace McGartland, *Thunderbolt Thinking* (Austin, Tex.: Bernard-Davis, 1994), 40. McGartland suggests that readers draw a picture of their brain. I adapted this to drawing a picture of your company.

[4]Chin-Ning Chu, *Thick Face Black Heart: The Path to Thriving, Winning & Succeeding* (Mill Valley, Calif.: AMC Publishing, 1992), 10–13.

Chapter 3

Know Thy Customer

Get your facts first, and then you are free to distort them as much as you please.

Mark Twain

Grill Your Customer

What do you associate with the term "outdoor barbecue grill"? Probably an ugly black iron box that requires a propane tank. What do you associate with the term "electric grill"? Probably a grill that cannot reach high enough temperatures to sear and brown what you're cooking.

In 1993 Thermos Company of Schaumburg, Illinois, introduced a product called the Thermal Electric Grill that combined the high-temperature capability of gas and charcoal grills with the convenience of electric grills. It promptly disrupted the marketplace that had been dominated by Weber and Char-Broil.

Before Thermos went about creating a new type of grill, it did an extraordinary amount of market research to get to know its customers. Reporter Brian Dumaine described the process in *Fortune*.[1] The first step was going into the field to conduct interviews and focus groups and to videotape consumers using grills. Thermos learned the following about the needs of its customers:

- People were tired of the mess of charcoal and the hassle of refilling propane tanks.

- People wanted a more attractive-looking barbecue that would complement the decor of their patios.

- Apartment and town-house residents had small balconies and patios that couldn't accommodate traditional full-size grills.

- Fire-prevention restrictions often prohibited apartment and town-house residents from using gas or charcoal barbecues.

- In parts of the country such as southern California, lighter fluid is banned because it contributes to air pollution.

The bottom line was that customers needed a radically new kind of barbecue. It had to get hot enough to sear meat, but it couldn't use gas or charcoal. And it had to be attractive—or at least blend in with the decor.

If Thermos had not gotten to know its customers, it might have designed yet another big, black barbecue. Instead, the design team did its homework, and Thermos produced a new product that was compact, attractive, and capable of reaching high temperatures.

Just as Honda knew itself and broadly applied its expertise in making engines, Thermos applied its expertise in insulation and heat transfer to achieve high grilling temperatures. Thermos's efforts created awareness of and demand for electric grills in a market traditionally dominated by gas and charcoal grills. Thermos's revenues grew approximately 13 percent in 1993 as the result of the electric grill and other new

---

Exercise

Pick the statement that most accurately describes your beliefs:

a. Market research is the process of estimating market size for the financial people.

b. Market research is the process of determining design requirements for engineers.

---

products. As further confirmation of its accomplishment, Thermos's competition was forced to bring out their own high-end electric grills.

Define Your Customers

U nlike knowing yourself, knowing your customer will take more than shutting your door and thinking about things. You must go into the field and press flesh. This is the kind of information you need to learn about your customer:

- Who is using and who is buying your product?

When the Thermos design team went into the field, they discovered that the stereotype of the man of the house doing the barbecuing was wrong. More and more women were the chefs, and they had different product expectations than men.

For example, women didn't like the messiness of charcoal or the inconvenience of replacing propane tanks. Uncovering the true users of grills indicated a need to focus on convenience and cleanliness.

Also, it's just as important to determine who is actually purchasing your product as well as knowing who is using it. For example, a toddler will be using a toy but a parent buys it, so packaging that screams "Educational!" (or "Indestructible!") is important.

- How are products in your category used by your customer?

The Thermos team saw that a large percentage of grills were being used on small patios and balconies of apartments. Also, many homeowners wanted grills that didn't mar the aesthetics of their decks.

When the Thermos team saw how grills were being used, the need for a compact and attractive industrial design became apparent. Old assumptions were thrown out as the team began to design a new customer-oriented grill. For example, the team designed a grill with three legs instead of the usual four so that it could fit into the corners of balconies.[2]

- Are laws, regulations, or societal pressures changing your marketplace?

When the Thermos team discovered that starter fluid was banned in some parts of the United States, it realized that charcoal grills were probably becoming more difficult to light. Also, consumers nationwide were less likely to purchase barbecues that generated large amounts of smoke because of the impact on the environment.

These kinds of environmental laws and concerns indicated that an electric grill had powerful advantages over gas and charcoal grills. However, the team also found out that people were dissatisfied with existing electric grills because these products could not achieve high temperatures. The final design achieved twice the temperature of most electric grills.[3]

The Art of Pressing Flesh

There's nothing fancy, expensive, or sophisticated about the process of getting to know your customers. Ninety percent of the process is a willingness to listen to your customers. The remaining 10 percent is pressing flesh—making contact with people. There are four styles of flesh-pressing: the ad hoc team, the corporate commitment, the open channel, and the scientific approach.

The Ad Hoc Team

The Thermos example illustrates one way to get to know your customer: form a team and send it into the field to meet with customers. The Thermos design team was ad hoc: it had a specific goal—creating a new grill—and worked only toward this short-term end.

The advantage of this method is that it allows you to solve big problems quickly because it is focused on one goal. You go out, get the information, come back, design the product, test it, make changes, and ship it. This method also preserves the fidelity of information because those who will implement it are those who are talking to the customers.

The disadvantage is that the project-team approach is often an after-the-fact, stopgap technique that represents a heroic effort to "get back in touch with the customer." The situation should not have gotten so bad in the first place that such intense solutions became necessary.

The Corporate Commitment

Remember the story back in Chapter 2 about Honda's starting with scooters and moving on to motorcycles and then cars? One victim of Honda's success with motorcycles in the United States was Harley-Davidson, the American motorcycle manufacturer based in Milwaukee, Wisconsin. But nothing bad has to last forever: Harley-Davidson has made a stunning comeback from the pounding it took from Honda and other Japanese motorcycle manufacturers during the 1970s.

One of the reasons for this recovery was a renewed corporate commitment to understanding its customers. For example, every employee, from the receptionist to the vice president of styling, Willie G. Davidson, goes to bike rallies to ride with customers and get firsthand feedback on Harley bikes.[4]

In addition, when people buy a Harley, they get a one-year membership to the Harley Owners Group (HOG). HOG membership includes a subscription to a bimonthly publication called *Hog Tales* as well as other benefits such as admission to company open houses, local and national rallies, and private HOG functions at which Harley-Davidson employees pump customers for feedback as well as fraternize and socialize.[5]

The advantage of an ongoing corporate commitment to stay in touch

---

Exercise

Call your company and ask if there is any organization, club, or users group for customers. Which of the following choices best describes your experience?

a. I had no idea we're this good.

b. I had no idea we're this bad.

c. Why do I work for this company?

d. I'm glad I did this exercise before my boss did.

---

with the customer is that it reduces the likelihood of being blindsided by changing tastes or a competitive product. It also bonds a company to its customers—making it more difficult for the competition to steal them away.

However, customers whom you're close to seldom give tough feedback—just as people hesitate to tell a close friend that he or she is doing something wrong. To combat this, set up a "council meeting" where several customers can give you feedback at once. There's candor, as well as safety, in numbers.

The Open Channel

A third way to know your customer is to create an open channel so that customers can easily contact you. For example, General Electric operates the GE Answer Center (800-626-2000), a toll-free, twenty-four-hour number on which company representatives answer questions about GE products.*

Roughly 25 percent of the calls the service receives are prepurchase calls. The other 75 percent of calls come from current GE customers who

---

*Helen Gracon, a beta tester of this book, was having problems with her stove when she read this section and decided to contact the Answer Center. She called at 10:30 on a Saturday morning and the service, according to her, was "a 10." The first thing the GE representative asked her was whether she had an ohmmeter—which she did.

want repair or maintenance information. GE started the Answer Center to "put a face on GE and to make a large, bureaucratic organization act like a small company," says Answer Center manager Bill Waers.

All of the center's representatives are trained to answer the most commonly asked questions about GE products. In addition, a small staff of former field technicians answers technical questions. In some cases, they assist customers who are attempting do-it-yourself repair jobs after a purchase has already been made.

GE advertises its 800 number in the phone book, at trade shows, on television, and in product literature. Customer complaints, concerns, and suggestions are all recorded and routed to the appropriate product manager.

The advantage of the open-channel method of knowing your customer is that it enables you to know your *potential* customer—as well as people who have already done business with you.

The Scientific Approach

The fourth method of knowing your customer is to use a scientific approach, such as audits, consulting studies, and focus groups. Northstar-at-Tahoe, the company that runs the ski resort of the same name, implemented the scientific approach by giving each member of its frequent-skier club a wristband with an electronic chip. When a skier touches the wristband to a scanner prior to making a run, a computer calculates and tracks the vertical feet for that run. The number of feet are recorded as points, which are treated like mileage in airline frequent-flyer programs.

In this way, the company learns which ski runs club members have used, when they used them, and how much each member skied during the season.* According to Judy Daniels, public relations director, the program also fosters customer goodwill as members work to accumulate points for gifts such as cappuccino, ski tune-ups, and ski lessons. "Our loyal customers bring friends to Northstar to gain points rather than ski in a different place every day," says Daniels.

---

*The member with the most vertical feet in the 1993–94 season skied 500,000 vertical feet. He was seventy-seven years old.

Northstar also uses information gathered by the sys
special promotions to increase usage during nonpeak times ,
age members to use runs that are not as busy. For example,
made Wednesdays, the lowest attendance day, a triple-poin

Despite my own background, I advise you not to fall ?
technology. The trapdoor of technology—a dependency on tne deus ex
machina—is that one can all too easily become method-oriented instead
of results-oriented. Using a piece of chalk and a blackboard, a company
that cares can know its customers better than a company that has the
greatest computer system in the world but doesn't care.

Exercise

Does this describe how research is transformed in your organization?

Customer	It is a crock of shit, and it stinks.
Researcher	It is a container of feces, and most unpleasant in smell.
Manager	It is an earthenware vessel of excrement, and it is very strong.
Director	It is a vase of fertilizer, and no one can resist its strength.
Vice President	It contains substances that aid plant growth, and it is very potent.
Chief Operating Officer	It promotes growth, and it is very robust.
President	Let's implement this terrific idea because it will promote growth.

Revolution Versus Evolution

Remember, the title of this chapter is Know Thy Customer, not Always Listen to Thy Customer. While it is important to know who your customers are and what they want, it is not always a good idea—it may even be detrimental—to do what they say.

Customers can usually describe what's wrong with what they own and the obvious ways to fix it. They are notoriously poor, however, at articulating what they *need* beyond their current frame of reference. I learned this lesson early in my career at Apple. At the time, the IBM PC running MS-DOS was the standard business personal computer. When we asked people what they wanted in a new computer, they answered only in terms of what they were already using or had already seen: a faster and cheaper MS-DOS machine.

They could not draw outside the lines and articulate what they *needed* in order to be more creative and more productive. (In a rare moment of humility, let me state that if you now asked Macintosh owners what they want, they would not be able to articulate their needs beyond a faster and cheaper Macintosh.)

It was our job to know our customers well enough to go beyond their articulated wants and produce a revolutionary new computer that served their unarticulated needs. After we started the revolution, we needed to listen to customers to learn how to evolve Macintosh. They told us—though we didn't listen well enough at first—that they wanted features such as an internal hard disk, slots, color, and faster networking.

There is a trick to listening to feedback: Avoid the extremes of "marketing mania," where you try to act on everything the customer says, and "paralysis through analysis," where you act on nothing. To strike the right balance, you need to tailor your research strategy to the level of uncertainty about your product's acceptability that you're facing.

The level of uncertainty, according to Bill Meade, a marketing professor at the University of Missouri at St. Louis, is a function of two factors: your understanding of the uses of your product and your ability to articulate unspoken customer needs. For example, when Macintosh was introduced, we had a poor understanding of how it would be used. Thus, we had a high level of uncertainty. Meade would have told us that the best way to get information was to ship it and see what happened. This table explains which type of research can best handle each level of uncertainty.

Level of Uncertainty	How to Get Valid Information	Research Method
Low—for example, milking a cash cow	Asking	Telephone and mail surveys
Medium—for example, upgrading a newly introduced product	Deriving	Debrief power users
High—for example, creating a new market	Prototyping	Take the shot

The lesson of this chapter is: Know your customers well enough to satisfy the needs they cannot even express. Then get to know your customers again to satisfy the changes and upgrades they can express. By following this formula, you can start and sustain a revolution.

Interview: David Kairys

David Kairys is a lawyer from Philadelphia. However, he is anything but a "Philadelphia lawyer." Kairys has practiced law for over twenty years with a small firm, Kairys & Rudovsky, and for the last five years has been a professor of constitutional law at Temple University School of Law. He is the author of many legal articles, newspaper columns, and two books, most recently, *With Liberty and Justice for Some*.

Kairys specializes in cases involving discrimination, free speech, and government misconduct. His opponents are usually large and formidable enemies such as the FBI and Philadelphia's city government. For example, he recently won a racial harassment case against the FBI, and he represented baby-doctor Benjamin Spock before the U.S. Supreme Court in a free-speech case.

Kairys was also one of the defense attorneys in the "Camden 28" case during the early 1970s. This case involved twenty-eight anti-Vietnam War protesters who raided and trashed a draft board office in Camden, New Jersey. Though there was no doubt that they committed the crime, a jury acquitted them of all charges after the government's action to *encourage* their actions via an informant came to light.

Philadelphia Magazine listed Kairys as one of the "Lawyers Who Drive Other Lawyers to Drink." The magazine described him in this way:

> Our Saint Jude. Has never met a hopeless case that failed to intrigue him. He uses the law to battle City Hall, red tape, and callous capitalism. A good lawyer, too. The chief of the city's small tribe of public interest lawyers.[7]

This interview illustrates how knowing your customer is as essential in the courtroom as it is in business. In Kairys's profession, the customer is the judge and jury.

Q: How did you win an acquittal for the Camden 28 when they were caught red-handed?

The trial became a combination of explaining the reasons why they opposed the war, educating the jury about the war, and emphasizing that the government, for its own political reasons, wanted this raid to happen so it could catch them in the act. The FBI had an informant in the group who provided the plans, tools, and other resources—who made it happen—at the taxpayer's expense. One of the reasons we were so effective is that the defendants spoke for themselves as well as through lawyers. They were humanized while the FBI's motives and tactics were challenged.

When we first did what we did, the judge wasn't happy, but over the course of a four-month trial things started to come out. We were willing to go against the grain: some of what we did is not a recognized defense, but the jury has a mandate to decide if someone's a criminal and if he deserves to be branded by the public as a criminal.

Good defense lawyers know that, and that's sometimes all you have to play to. If you convince the jurors that the defendants are not really criminals and should not be branded by the people as criminals, they will tend to acquit. The prosecution started out by spending over a month proving that the defendants raided the draft board and tore up all the records. We started out the case by saying that this was all true and irrelevant. It drove the prosecution nuts.

Q: How can you tell who will be a good customer—aka, juror?

Jurors in highly publicized cases are going to know something about the cases, and it's usually going to be negative from the defense's perspective. Also, most people believe that if the police arrested somebody and the prosecutors decided to charge him, he is probably guilty. The Perry Mason syndrome is a real problem, too. People think that if someone is innocent, the guy who really did it will jump up at the end and admit it. I never had a case with a person who jumped up!

Recognizing all this, we started doing some research—now we might call it "marketing research." A creative sociologist named Jay Schulmann put together a survey for the Harrisburg prosecution of the Berrigan brothers. They were charged by J. Edgar Hoover with trying to blow up the heating tunnels in Washington, D.C., and plotting to assassinate Henry Kissinger. The prosecution chose Harrisburg, Pennsylvania, because it was known as one of the most conservative places in the world.

The shoot-from-the-hip rules that lawyers use to figure out which jurors might be good for the defense were almost all wrong. For instance, reading *The New York Times* was seen as a sign of liberalism—or openness to listen to the defense. But the correlation went the other way: our survey showed that people who read *The New York Times* were among the most pro-prosecution.

When we investigated further, it appeared that *The New York Times* was the only paper available in Harrisburg that had the stock quotes, and nobody else read it but the people who had invested in the stock market—which, in Harrisburg, was a very conservative group of people.

The survey also showed that high-school graduates were a little more open to the defense than college graduates. The usual assumption was the more education, the more liberal, so lawyers all over the country were picking college graduates over high-school graduates. This is like a business modeling its appeal in the exact opposite way of what your market is. Most people who went away and got a liberal arts education never came back to Harrisburg. High-school graduates were a random assortment of people, which included liberals.

The most crucial factor wasn't anything that you'd even call liberal or conservative. We looked for open-minded people who didn't think in an authoritarian way. We weren't going to get jurors who were in favor of blowing up the tunnels in Washington, D.C. We wanted the kind of person who says, "Well, show me. I'm not going to accept that and put my co-citizen in jail just because you say so, and I'm not afraid to go home if I vote for acquittal."

Lawyers are educated to, and tend to, think that you win or lose on the legally defined issues and facts, but the jury is going to make the decision. Lawyers regularly ignore this. Lawyers know juries are immensely unpredictable, which is why most cases settle out of court. Many an experienced lawyer has been shocked after being certain that your side had the better of it. Later, when you talk to the jurors, you find out that they may have focused on some little thing that was said the first afternoon that you didn't think meant a thing, but it became a big thing to them. Lawyers are afraid of jurors!

Q: Just like companies are afraid of customers?

Absolutely, and big law firms are the most afraid of juries. Most partners of big, prestigious law firms became partners without ever having done a jury trial.

This is an advantage for the little guy who has to do every phase of a case because there's nobody else. I was there during every deposition. I know every word that was said. I have a memory of all the details and all the nuances. If you let one lawyer take the depositions who has no trial experience and in many ways doesn't know the right questions to ask, and then turn over the huge file of paper to the trial wizard, the trial wizard won't know what's going on.

Q: What about the other customer called the judge?

Law schools and most lawyers think that the judge is going to want to know that the precedents and law are on your side and want to hear a brilliant legal argument. However, if you are representing underdogs, the most important thing is to have the judge believe in his gut that an injustice was done. Then legal theories even on the fringe can work.

Also, lawyers always talk about judges. They'll say that so and so judge is a liberal on search issues, but he hates gun cases, so if you're a criminal lawyer and you've got a person charged with possession of a big gun, you're going to get creamed by this judge. All these things are known about each of the judges and are a source of constant scuttlebutt among lawyers.

Now there are also more sophisticated ways. You can use the computerized research networks like LEXIS and Westlaw. You can just run a judge's name through, and you'll get every decision they made that's published.

You've got to assess the judge and figure out what matters to the judge. Sometimes there isn't a good opening, but it might matter most to the judge, for instance, that all the Democratic committeemen in your town are for your side. That may be the most important thing you could prove, or say.

Q: How could you possibly bring this up in a trial?

You've got to be creative. You've got to make it relevant. If it's some kind of voting issue, you have the head of the city committee come in as a witness even if the court doesn't let him testify. You make what's called an offer of proof. The judge can rule it irrelevant, but the judge has heard it.

Q: Is a trial attorney a "sales" person who "performs" in court?

Courtroom performance matters, but I think it's overplayed. It feels great when you cross-examine the witness who is left with his jaw open, and I'm certainly not immune to that feeling. But sometimes you destroy the witness and the jury feels sorry for him. You don't know the effect of various things you do, and sometimes you have to restrain your feelings to vanquish the enemy.

You've got to do a lot of homework. You've got to investigate like crazy. See where there are openings for your viewpoint. Investigate all of the people who are going to make the decision, and think out strategies as to how you're going to convince them.

Think about your opponent. What's your opponent going to do? How are you going to counter what your opponent does? What things might your opponent do that might help you so that you want to encourage him to do them? It's very strategic. But, in the wins that I feel the greatest about, I'm not sure if all the planning and all the strategy means as much as the substance of what's going on and how the decision-makers perceive it.

Q: So a trial comes down to focusing on customers and creating good products—as opposed to "sales"?

Jurors believe what they believe, and they understand it the way they understand it—whether you brought it home in an incredibly sophisticated way or they figured it out without you. The most important things a lawyer can project might just be honesty and integrity—and a little humor once in a while. Then if you've done the research, thought out your strategies, and determined a clear, consistent approach—and if you believe in what you're doing—the theatrics probably won't matter much.

Notes

[1]Brian Dumaine, "Payoff from the New Management," *Fortune*, 13 December 1993, 103.

[2]Karen E. Klages, "Simple Pleasures and Lovers of Comfort Win Big in Annual Good Design Competition," *Chicago Tribune*, 22 May 1994, 3.

[3]Ibid.

[4]Stan Rapp and Thomas Collins, *Beyond MaxiMarketing: The New Power of Caring and Daring* (New York: McGraw-Hill, Inc., 1994), 96.

[5]Peter Reid, *Well Made in America: Lessons from Harley-Davidson on Being the Best* (New York: McGraw-Hill Publishing Company, 1990), 91–92, 193–94.

[6]"Frequent-Skier Program Should Pay for Itself in First Two Years," *Colloquy* 3, No. 4 (1992), 1, 4–5.

[7]Mike Marlowe with Sara Sklaroff, "The Philadelphia Lawyer—An Operator's Manual," *Philadelphia*, November 1990, 104.

Chapter 4

Know Thy Enemy

We were fairly arrogant, until we realized the Japanese were selling quality products for what it cost us to make them.

Paul Allaire, president of Xerox

"Meeting the Competition"

A chapter in Sam Walton's book, *Made in America*, is called "Meeting the Competition." In this section, Walton, the late chairman of Wal-Mart, the Bentonville, Arkansas, retailer he started, explains how he competed with companies like Kmart and Price Club.

I suspect Walton meant "meeting" in the sense of *veni, vidi, vici.**

*In case you studied a language you could use, instead of Latin, this translates to "I came, I saw, I conquered."

However, he also literally "met" the competition to see firsthand what they were doing. For example, in the early 1950s when Walton heard about a new retailing concept called self-service, he traveled by bus from Arkansas to Minnesota to visit two Ben Franklin stores where the concept had been implemented.[1]

Much later—and richer—Walton frequently roamed Kmart stores with a tape recorder, asking questions of its employees because he considered Kmart his laboratory. At the time, Kmart had five hundred stores, which accounted for $3 billion in sales, while Wal-Mart had approximately sixty stores and sales of $80 million.

To learn about superstores, Walton studied Price Club. In his book, he recounts an episode when he was dictating notes about prices and merchandising to a tape recorder in a Price Club store. An employee told Walton that he would have to erase what he recorded because Price Club didn't allow the use of tape recorders in the store.

Walton was caught red-handed, and he knew it. Wal-Mart had the same policy, so Walton didn't protest, but he wrote a note to Robert Price, the founder's son. In the note Walton explained that there was material that didn't deal with Price Club, and he would like to have that part of the tape returned. A few days later when Walton got the tape back from Robert Price, nothing had been erased. Walton admits in his book, "He probably treated me better than I deserved."

What can we learn from Sam Walton's methods?

- Competitive research starts at the top. It isn't something to delegate to underlings, the marketing department, or consultants. In many companies it seems the closer you are to the competition (or the customer!), the lower your status. Walton was the CEO, and he did his own research.

- The best researcher is often the person who is going to use the information to make decisions. This person can see nuances and traps that escape others. Also, the decision-maker can cross-fertilize. For example, while studying prices, he or she may notice a point-of-purchase display idea.

- Competitive research isn't hard or necessarily expensive. For many organizations, it just means getting out of your chair, getting in a car or plane, and seeing what the competition is doing. Common sense and hustle are more important than money.

- Don't be proud. Walton readily admits copying Kmart as he built up Wal-Mart. He admits he copied Price Club when he started Sam's Club. If you see a good idea, adapt it to your own needs but also be aware that part of being a good thief is knowing what to steal.

- Use a small tape recorder.

E x e r c i s e

When was the last time you shopped your competition?

Define Your Competition's Identity

Walton was a Yoda-like figure when it came to competitive research. Figuring out what the competition was doing and what to copy was probably second nature to him. But how can the rest of us reach this enlightened state?

First, be thorough. Many companies concentrate on side-by-side feature comparisons of products and stop there. However, the product with the most features may lose in the marketplace because people buy things for reasons that often don't show up on feature lists—for example, a company's reputation for service and support. It pays to examine all the benefits of doing business with your competition.

Second, adjust your radar. Many companies only consider large, established companies as their competition. They don't look for companies that are flying low, flying high, or coming in from an unexpected direction. Benjamin Gilad, a management professor at Rutgers University, puts it this way:

> Large companies pay attention to large companies (or to large consulting firms who pay attention to large companies).[2]

Honda, for example, flew under the radar of the American car industry when it entered the U.S. market. A good competitive analysis includes an examination of the policies and perspectives of your competition—large and small, old and new, local and distant. Then and only then can you get the full measure of your enemy.

Being complete and adjusting your radar will enable you to identify your current and future competition. Then you can undertake the process of examining big-picture, conceptual issues as well as the nitty-gritty details of how your competition operates. Big-picture issues include:

- What is your competition's mission? What are your competition's goals and objectives?

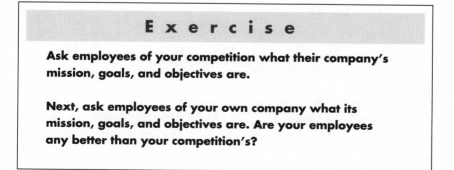

- Does your competition consider itself market, product, or service driven?

- Does your competition consider itself your competition?

- What are your competition's strengths and weaknesses?

- Is your competition a contented cow, a leader, an upstart, or a guerrilla?

The most difficult aspect of obtaining this kind of information is not that employees consider it confidential—they simply don't know it. Also, different parts of your competitor may act like different companies, so examine the part you compete with.

Moving from big-picture issues, nitty-gritty details involve the day-to-day operation of your competition.

- What channels does your competition use to distribute its products?

- How does your competition position its products?

- How does your competition create new products?

- How does your competition manufacture its products?

- What are your competition's pricing, discount, payment terms, and rebate policies?

- How does your competition handle customer service and returns?

- How does your competition solicit customer feedback?

Profile the Competition's Executives

When a football team prepares to play an opponent, it analyzes its opponent's strategies ("They like to establish a running game to open up the passing game") and tactics ("They run outside because of the speed of their backs").

One aspect of competitive research that football teams are better at than businesses is in profiling the key players of the opposition. Before each game, football teams post pictures of key players along with an analysis of their strengths and weaknesses. Business can learn from how football teams operate, so answer these questions:

- Who are the key players on your competitor's team?

- What are their educational and professional backgrounds?

- What are their strengths and weaknesses? What are their hot buttons? What makes them "tick"?

E x e r c i s e

Obtain photographs of the executives of your competition. Ask your managers to identify as many as they can.*

Anticipate Your Competition's Response

The final area to study is your competition's likely responses to your actions, actions of other companies, and changes in the industry. You need to anticipate how fast your competition will react and what kind of actions they will take. These questions help to clarify your competition's probable response:

- Is the company internally or externally focused?

Internally focused companies are often referred to as "process driven"or "engineering driven." They are slow to notice changes in the marketplace. They might also be described as arrogant and living in an ivory tower.

---

*The results of this exercise will depress you.

- How does information get transmitted within the company?

Competition that has a tall hierarchy with rigid lines of communication will transmit information slowly—if at all. Ever play the game where each person passes on a whispered message until the last person says what he or she has heard? The results are usually hilarious, except in business, where they're tragic.

- Who interprets the data?

A manager who has been through years of price wars will interpret an opponent's price reduction differently from a Harvard MBA, who's never been closer to a price war than a lecture hall, or a Wharton MBA, who has to formulate an econometric model to buy a pack of gum. Therefore, examine the educational background and experience of your competition's executives.

- What "drives" your competition?

Most companies have one of four goals: gross sales, net profit, ego bolstering, or strategic advances. A gross-sales–oriented company may sacrifice profits and fight for sales. A net-profit–oriented company will only go so far to match the competition. A company run on egos may react violently and uncontrollably. A strategic company may be willing to compete for long-term position.[3]

Techniques to Know Thy Enemy

A restaurant called Chef Allen's in North Miami Beach, Florida, operates a program called Chow Now Scholarship. Every employee—servers, cooks, and dishwashers on up—receives $50 to dine at similar restaurants to learn about the competition. After conducting the "research," the servers and cooks prepare a short written report and make an oral presentation about what they learned.[4]

E x e r c i s e

Before you go on, take this test. To analyze my competition, I always:

a. **Shop the competition**

b. **Become a customer of the competition**

c. **Query the competition's customers**

d. **Read voraciously and omnivorously**

e. **Attend conferences, trade shows, and association meetings**

f. **Ask the government about the competition**

g. **Suck up to a research librarian**

h. **Get on the Internet and search for my competition's Web page**

0–2: You're a bozo. 3–5: You're okay. 6–8: You can skip this section. 9: You better learn how to count.

Chef Allen's illustrates that knowing your enemy is mostly a caring attitude for your customer—not a budget line item for a fancy market research firm. (Chef Allen's competitive research efforts are part of a general drive-your-competition-crazy attitude: the restaurant also has a policy of calling the host of dinner parties of eight or more the day after the dinner.[5])

Whether you run a restaurant, a nationwide retailer, or a one-person consulting firm, here are ways to check out your competition.

▪ Pull a Walton

Pretend you are a customer and see how your competition markets, sells, and services its product. Go to its store. Order its catalog. Ask for its price list. Request its brochure. See how your competition sells against your company. Gather all the promotional literature you can for analysis.

▪ Become a customer of your competition

Not only should you shop your competition, you should buy its product to become its customer. This will give you an opportunity to examine after-sale support, service, and follow-up sales efforts. Your competition may also have publications for customers that are full of tidbits.

▪ Become an investor in your competition

If your competition is a publicly traded company, one of the easiest ways to get information about it is to buy a share of its stock. This entitles you to receive shareholder information about the company such as quarterly and annual reports.

▪ Query your competition's customers

Your competition's customers are a great source of information. Draw the line, however, at violating good ethics and obtaining confidential information, even if it's offered to you. Note: anyone who will violate your competition's confidentiality will violate yours, too.

▪ Read voraciously and omnivorously

Read everything you can about your industry and your competition in books, magazines, and trade rags. Read the local paper of your competitors' hometowns. Read scientific journals, because your competition's research- ers may release highly technical information in these specialized publica- tions.

If you don't have the time to read omnivorously (though I know that you do), then install magazine racks in your company's bathrooms, place the publications you want read in the racks, and instruct employees to tear out pertinent articles and place them in a "competition box" for dissemination to the rest of the company.

▪ Attend conferences, trade shows, and association meetings

Most people like to impress the audience at these kinds of events, and may leak information to do so. Listen to the speeches of your competition's management to learn about its strategic directions. Be sure to shop your competition's booths at shows.

▪ Ask the government

Your competition often must make disclosures to federal, state, and local government agencies for public offerings, government bids, tax assessment, building permits, patent and trademark registration, and requests for subsidies and benefits. These are almost always a matter of public record and contain information about a company's goals, strategies, and technology.

▪ Suck up to a research librarian (or become your own)

Find a good librarian and endear yourself to him or her.* By using a combination of books (*Who's Who in Finance and Industry*) and online services (LEXIS-NEXIS) to search local newspapers, these professionals can do more in five minutes than you can do in a day.

Becoming your own research librarian is also getting easier and easier. By joining a computer online service such as America Online or CompuServe, you can search through past issues of many newspapers, magazines, and journals.

Also, unless you've been living under a rock, you've heard of the Internet. Many companies, both large and small, maintain areas on the Internet where they provide information about themselves and their products. These are called Web pages.

To utilize an online service and to check your competition's Web page, you need a moderate amount of equipment: a computer,† a modem, and some software—an expense of about $1,500 at 1995 prices.

*I hear they like fountain pens.
†I strongly recommend that you buy a Macintosh unless you want to drive *yourself* crazy.

Exercise

The Muns Test

Pretend that Guy Kawasaki is the vice president of marketing of your competition. Find out all you can about him.

A research librarian at the University of Missouri, St. Louis, named Raleigh Muns provided a solution for this exercise. His answer is provided at the end of this chapter for you to compare your results to.

Chapters 2, 3, and 4 helped you build a base of knowledge about your organization, customers, and enemy. Armed with this knowledge, you're ready to take action. Before we go, however, the following interview explains how to use this kind of knowledge to create bleeding-edge advertising.

Interview: Allen Kay

I f you're into computers, the name Alan Kay may ring a bell. He's one of the folks from Xerox PARC who created much of the technology of graphical user interfaces, mice, and laser printers. But if you have anything to do with advertising, you've heard of another Allen Kay. This one is associated with controversial and effective head-to-head advertising campaigns.

The advertising Allen Kay created for the Xerox high-speed duplicator in the mid-seventies featured a monk named Brother Dominick.* In the campaign, Brother Dominick is shown in the basement of an abbey laboriously writing a manuscript. When he's done, Father Superior asks for five hundred more sets. Luckily, Brother Dominick has a friend with a Xerox duplicator, so he can fulfill the request.

---

*Brother Dominick was played by Jack Eagle, a former big-band trumpet player and comic who is Jewish. He used to describe himself as the world's only Jewish monk— a "schmonk."

Kay is the founder of Korey, Kay & Partners, a $75-million advertising agency in New York City. Prior to founding his company, he was senior vice president/creative director of Needham, Harper & Steers, New York (now called DDB Needham). He's won numerous awards including eighteen Clios, the *Lion D'or* at the Cannes Film Festival, and six *Fortune* magazine "Best Read Advertising" awards.

His ads, in his words, try to "outsmart the outspenders." Among his current clients are Virgin Atlantic Airways, Celebrity Cruises, Members Only, Comedy Central, BayBank, and the Metropolitan Transportation Authority of New York. In this interview he explains how to use advertising as a weapon to drive your competition crazy.

Q: What kind of advertising can a company use against its competitors in a head-to-head battle?

When you're going head-to-head with a competitor, there are two approaches to take. One we call "Achilles' Heel," and the other we call "King of the Hill." In Achilles' Heel advertising, you find out the competitor's weakness, and you combat it with your strengths.

The first time I used Achilles' Heel advertising was in the mid-seventies. Procter & Gamble had just come out with a product called Pringles, which they positioned as the newfangled potato chip. They began in California, were extremely successful, and started moving across the country.

We were working for Wise Potato Chips. It was the most popular potato chip in the New York area, but the Wise people were shaking in their boots. Out of curiosity, we got the Pringles package, and that was the beginning of the end. It read like a chemistry set—with things like mono- and diglycerides and butylated hydroxyanisole—to preserve freshness of all things!

Then we looked at Wise's packaging, and their ingredients were potatoes, vegetable oil, and salt. It was just at the beginning of the health food craze, so this was fabulous. It was all we needed. Pringles gave us the ammunition needed to do the job we had to do.

We created a very simple commercial: two women sitting side by side. In front of one woman was a can of Pringles and in front of the other woman was a bag of Wise potato chips. The woman with the Pringles picks up the can and reads the long list of chemical ingredients. Then the other woman picks up the Wise package and reads, "Wise potato chips contains potatoes, vegetable oil, and salt." Then we cut to Pringles and the announcer says, "The newfangled potato chip." We cut to Wise and he says, "Or Wise, the oldfangled potato chip. You decide."

Wise's sales stayed the same or did a little better, but the main thing was that Pringles took none of Wise's business. The word got out, and the next thing you know, all across the country local chippers were doing their versions of our campaign. Just as Pringles rolled across the country, they rolled back across the country after our ads, and Procter & Gamble pulled the product for reformulation.

Q: What is an example of King-of-the-Hill advertising?

In King-of-the-Hill advertising you find out the competitor's strength and present yourself as being stronger at it. British Airways was the gold standard in San Francisco. We wanted to tell people as much as we could about Virgin Atlantic Airways in as short a period of time. Virgin was a relatively unknown quantity in San Francisco.

People knew British Airways had good-quality products; so did Virgin. They knew British Airways had regular flights and big airplanes; so did Virgin. Therefore, if we could quickly put ourselves on the same pedestal as British Air, we would get considered.

So the advertising started with a teaser that appeared on billboards and on television with the phrase "Yoooooo-hoooooo, British Aiiiiirrrr-wayyys," which signaled, Uh-oh, somebody's coming to compete with British Airways. It was the shortcut to the top of the mountain. The customer knew that there was going to be someone new in town. They had a frame of reference even before they knew the name of the product.

Q: So you positioned Virgin against the standard?

Exactly. We understood the standard, so we telegraphed all the key attributes of Virgin. Soon after the teaser campaign, we put the Virgin logo on that ad and the rest of the advertising. By the time people saw Virgin advertising, they knew that Virgin was an airline that flew to London. It was very high quality, and it was competing with British Airways, so it must be pretty damn good.

Then people wanted to find out how good Virgin was, so the advertising told people about the limousine service, the videos at every seat, the first-class lounge, etc., etc. All we had to do was concentrate on communicating why we were better than British Airways rather than explaining what Virgin Atlantic was about in the first place. We hit the ground flying, so to speak.

Q: How do you develop this kind of advertising?

You have to know yourself and your competition equally well, and you have to know the customer—we always say start with the customer. We have five basic guidelines for developing advertising: Start with the customer. Live with the client. Uncover the obvious. Keep it simple. And follow through.

If you do each of these five things, you're going to come pretty damn close to the target. I always believe the problem will dictate the solution if you really understand the problem and set your objective.

Q: What is the best way to drive your competition crazy?

Continually doing what is best for your customers. That will always keep your competition guessing. If you keep your eyes on the prize, and you always do what is best for your company, things that you do will always be changing, but your strategy will be the same.

We don't do things to hurt British Airways. We don't do things to drive them crazy. That just happens to be the result, but that's not our intent. We can't get rich by making British Airways crazy. We get rich by filling up airplanes.

Answer to the Muns Test

This is what Raleigh Muns found when I asked him to do a background search on me. Notice that he suggests a five-step research plan. Raleigh can be reached at his email address: fugitive @crl.com.

Applied to Guy Kawasaki on January 16, 1995.

Step 1. Ask your local librarian to do it.

The Library of Congress Catalog lists four books by Guy Kawasaki. The catalog also lists his date of birth as 1954. (Doctoral dissertations, and less often, masters theses may also be located by a good librarian.)

Database 101. Berkeley: Peachpit, ©1991.
The Macintosh Way. Glenview, Ill.: Scott, Foresman, ©1990.
Selling the Dream. N.Y.: HarperBusiness, ©1992.
Hindsights. Hillsboro, Ore.: Beyond Words, ©1993.

Step 2. Use your local library's "biography" guides.

No Guy: *Biography and Genealogy Master Index*. Detroit: Gale, 1990.

No Guy: *Who's Who in Finance and Industry*. Chicago: Marquis, 1994.

No Guy: *Who's Who Among Asian Americans*. Detroit: Gale, 1994.*

Step 3. Look for local newspaper sources and local business directories.

San Francisco Examiner (4/17/94; p. B1). Donates $500 to playground.

*I guess I'm not a very important Asian American.

Step 4. Get online with LEXIS-NEXIS.

Searching for the phrase "Guy Kawasaki" turned up 345 articles. (Searching for a relative unknown like "Raleigh Muns" will turn up three articles.) Here are some of the highlights:

New York Times (5/2/1993; Sec. 3, p. 11)

Born August 30, 1954, Honolulu; lives in San Francisco; read "Charlie's Victory" by Charlie and Lucy Wedemeyer; drives (in 1993) a 1992 Acura NSX; B.A. Psychology (Stanford); M.B.A. from UCLA; married to Beth Thomsen Kawasaki; has one son; joined Apple in 1983 as Macintosh software Evangelist; promoted to director of software product management in 1987; quit two weeks later to help start software company called ACIUS, Inc.

MacWEEK (10/24/89; p. 26)

Quits ACIUS; ". . . life in silicon valley will be a little less interesting while Kawasaki is away."

Boston Globe (5/9/94; p. 49)

Awarded special "Father of the UGLYs" from Boston Computer Society.

Industry Week (11/7/94; p. 44)

Charges $10K for speaking.

Sales & Marketing Management (7/94; p. 101)

Selling the Dream on summer reading list of Phil Maez, vice president of sales at Celestial Seasoning, Inc.

Network World (4/4/94)

Self-description quote: "High-tech men are body by Volkswagen, brains by Cray, heart by Frigidaire, personality by Metamucil."

Step 5: Use an information broker.

Try "Information Brokers" in the Yellow Pages. Local libraries may also maintain lists of local brokers. For the adventurous with access to the Internet, use the World Wide Web to connect to

http://www.commerce.net/directories/consultants.html

and search the consultants listing using the term "information brokering" for possible hits. Information brokers will charge steeper fees than a librarian ($50/hour and up versus "free") but will have access to more resources, be able to apply focused expertise, and you won't have to wait in line!

Notes

[1]Sandra S. Vance and Roy V. Scott, *Wal-Mart: A History of Sam Walton's Retail Phenomenon* (New York: Twayne Publishers, 1994), 11–12.

[2]Benjamin Gilad, *Business Blindspots* (Chicago: Probus Publishing Company, 1994), 21.

[3]Ken Smith, Curtis Brimm, and Martin Gannon, *Dynamics of Competitive Strategy* (Newbury Park, Calif.: Sage Publications, Inc., 1992), 91–119.

[4]Susan Greco, ed., "Hands On Sales and Marketing," *Inc.*, October 1994, 119.

[5]Susan Greco, "Real-World Customer Service," *Inc.*, October 1994, 40.

Part Two

Do the

Right Things

Want to know the biggest non-secret in business? The best way to drive your competition crazy is to do the right things. If you do the right things, you will relegate all comers to the slippery slope toward lunacy. What are these things? Part II provides the answers:

- Take such damn good care of customers that they have no choice but to do business with you (Chapter 5, Focus on Your Customers).

- Toss out vanity, superficiality, and irrelevance and do what really matters (Chapter 6, Concentrate on a Decisive Point).

- View your customers not as pain-in-the-ass patrons but as potential (unpaid!) salespeople (Chapter 7, Turn Customers into Evangelists).

- Do something good for society (Chapter 8, Make Good by Doing Good).

Focus on Your Customers

My way of fighting the competition is the positive approach. Stress your own strengths, emphasize quality, service, cleanliness, and value, and the competition will wear itself out trying to keep up.

Ray Kroc, founder and late chairman of McDonald's

Two Personal Examples

Pigs will floss before this maxim changes: The best way to drive your competition crazy is to make your customers happy. To make your customers happy, you have to focus on them. And if you always focus on your customers, you may never need to fire a shot at your competition, and you don't need to read the rest of this book.

Here's how two very different companies—one a major hotel chain, the other an independent restaurant—acted on this principle and made their customers happy and their competition suffer.

First, on a trip to Hawaii in 1993, my wife, son, and I stayed in the Hyatt Regency Hotel in Poipu Beach, Kauai. I was amazed to see that there were free washers and dryers in the laundry rooms. Someone had truly thought about the customer's needs—in our case to wash an endless stream of bibs and baby clothes.

Few hotels would even consider laundry rooms—probably because they take up space and reduce the amount of revenue that hotel-done laundry generates, but the decision to make the washers and dryers free is monumental.

By focusing on the needs of its customers rather than nickel-and-diming them, the Kauai Hyatt communicates something of tremendous importance in the very competitive Hawaii hotel market: a general caring attitude. And it has turned me into an evangelist for the place.

E x e r c i s e

Check if there's a laundry room the next time you stay in a hotel. If there is, check if the washers and dryers are free. If they are, send me an email (Macway@aol.com) or fax (415-921-2479), so I can add it to my database of customer-focused hotels.

Second, on another trip I visited a restaurant called Old Wives' Tales in Portland, Oregon. I found out about it by asking an employee at a nearby Residence Inn to recommend a kid-friendly restaurant. His response: "You should go to the one with a playroom." My reaction: "Playroom? Tell me more." (Lesson: When you have a unique product or service, it's easier for people to remember you.)

The owner of the restaurant, Holly Hart, created the playroom because she noticed that people had a devil of a time dining out with kids. The playroom is about 130 square feet and contains three boats, a train, and a tunnel for kids to climb in, over, around, and through. Her efforts, however, go beyond the playroom. For example, as soon as you're seated, the waiter or waitress brings orange slices for your kids and extra napkins.

Hart has redefined the eating-out experience for parents. The historic choices are a short, miserable meal at a full-menu restaurant or an unsatisfying meal at a fast-food franchise with a playground. Like the Kauai Hyatt's, Hart's customer focus entails sacrifices: the playroom takes up the space of twenty revenue-generating seats, and the restaurant has less turnover of sittings because people stay longer since their kids are happy.

The children's play area at Old Wives' Tales.

The sacrifices are worth it, though, because Hart has increased business every year for fifteen straight years and is currently doing $1.5 million of business a year. Also, Hart has built up a loyal customer base that continues to eat there even after their kids have grown up. This is true despite the fact that Old Wives' Tales is located in a remote area so customers have to get in their cars and drive to it.

Ask the Right Questions

Focusing on beating the competition instead of focusing on the customer inevitably leads to tit-for-tat combat. Tit-for-tat combat inevitably leads to doing the wrong things for the seemingly right reasons.

Exercise

Go to a full-menu restaurant with your kids and time how long your dinner lasts before you have to—and want to—leave. (FYI, my family's dinner at Old Wives' Tales lasted one hour and thirty minutes—roughly one hour longer than usual.)

Extra credit: As soon as you're seated, ask for orange slices for your kids.

Instead, you should ask the right questions. For example, Holly Hart of Old Wives' Tales asked the right question: How can I redefine the dining experience for people?

Kenichi Ohmae, former director of the Tokyo office of the international firm of McKinsey & Company, provides another example of asking the right question. His right question led to the creation of a new class of photographic equipment called "point-and-shoot" cameras.

In the mid-seventies, single lens reflex (SLR) cameras zoomed in popularity because of their advanced features and flexibility. Many camera manufacturers were convinced that the way to succeed was to create better and better SLR cameras.

But Ohmae was not convinced by this conclusion, and asked two more questions: "Why do people take pictures in the first place?" and "What are they really looking for when they take pictures?"

He realized that people did not want good *cameras* as much as they wanted good *pictures*. So, Ohmae and his crew went to a film lab and looked at a sample of eighteen thousand pictures to analyze why pictures came out bad. They uncovered three main reasons:

- Poor adjustment for distances

- Insufficient light

- Incorrect f-stop settings for film speed and type

Basically, they learned that bad pictures were the result of human error. These and other findings inspired the creation of point-and-shoot cameras with automatic focus, built-in flashes, and automatic recognition of the type of film used.

Because Ohmae asked the right questions, lens-shutter camera manufacturers focused on the right issues for their customers. As a rule of thumb, asking the right question involves probing for salient *benefits*, not the gonzo *features*. Rather than joining the herd producing SLRs, these manufacturers created cameras that delivered what their customers wanted: good pictures with no guesswork.[1]

Provide Imaginative Solutions

E ventide Lutheran Home asked the right questions about what people wanted in a nursing home. It found that folks living in nursing homes often face lives of loneliness, isolation, and boredom. Eventide Lutheran Home, based in Moorhead, Minnesota, provided an imaginative solution to the needs of their customers by adopting the look and feel of a small town.

At this facility there's a post office with antique mailboxes, a gift shop with antique furnishings and a nineteenth-century candy dispenser, plus a bank, library, beauty parlor, barbershop, and soda shop. The residents elect one of their members as mayor, and the mayor convenes a town council to discuss resident concerns and brings those concerns to management.

Community organizations such as the Rotary Club, blood bank, heart association, and churches hold their meetings in the "town." The organizations are not charged for meeting space, and pay nominal rates for meals served in a dining hall. Local businesspeople often visit the low-priced café for lunch, and some families hold birthday parties at the soda shop.

Helen Frampton, president of Eventide, describes her customers: "They don't see awfulness, they see normal life. They come in knowing they will stay as active as possible." Eventide is proof that when you focus on your customer, imaginative solutions arise.

The "town hall" of Eventide Lutheran Home.

Break Down the Bunkers

Many companies force customers to climb over barriers to do business. This is the bunker theory of sales, marketing, and service: The customer is out in the trenches and the company employee is behind a bunker. The focus is on the company's, not the customer's, convenience.

E x e r c i s e

Call your company and try to get information about your products or services. Would you do business with your own company?

This attitude may seem great for the company: employees can sit at desks and let the customers come to them. If there are more customers than employees, the customers can wait in line. On the other hand, it isn't

64

anywhere close to great for customers who are made to feel that doing business with you is an honor and privilege.

Here are four illustrations of how companies broke down the bunkers:

- Mervyn's, a retailer based in Hayward, California, rolls portable sales terminals into a busy department to reduce customer waiting. Furthermore, once a month Mervyn's has a giant sale called Super Saturday. These days are extremely busy—often shoppers line up before the store opens—so Mervyn's uses a portable stand to verify non-Mervyn's credit cards while the shoppers wait in line.

- Blue Cross and Blue Shield of Massachusetts opened 1,000-square-foot information and service centers in two malls in Massachusetts. "We made a decision to meet our members and potential members where they are," says Dr. Joseph Avellone, chief operating officer of Blue Cross and Blue Shield of Massachusetts.

  Shoppers have access to ten staffers who can answer questions about existing policies for current members and provide information to prospective members. The centers also have interactive databases with information on diseases, Blue Cross products, and upcoming community health events.[2]

- The Bank of Boulder in Colorado doesn't dictate to customers when they can do business. Its solution is not just automated teller machines. This bank's idea of "banker's hours" is tellers working from 6 A.M. to 11 P.M. at drive-up windows.

  Although only 6 percent of the bank's customers use the service, 16 percent of new customers choose the bank because of the extended hours. Merchants making night deposits feel safer when there is a teller who can report any suspicious people instead of having just an isolated automated teller machine or deposit slot.[3]

- According to the *Wall Street Journal*, Toyota sells two out of every five cars in Japan. One of the reasons for its success is that it has 100,000 door-to-door salespeople who call on customers in their homes. Dealerships are actually used as bases of operation from which the sales force fans out and pounds the pavement.[4]

Each of these companies either made it easy for their customers to get to them or actually went to their customers. While their methods may not apply directly to your business, it's more important to embrace the *attitude* behind their efforts. As Allen Kay pointed out, you don't need to set out to drive your competition crazy. With the proper customer-focused attitude, however, you can hardly avoid it.

Provide a Complete Product

P art of the joy of buying something is taking home the product, ripping open the package, and being able to use it immediately, because you didn't need to buy accessories like batteries. Including everything needed to use a product is another way to focus on the customer.

Companies that take this simple step often produce significant product improvements. For example, Vasque, a hiking boot manufacturer in Red Wing, Minnesota, provides a small brush with its boot-cleaning solution.

Standard Brands, a paint company from Torrance, California, sells a promotional kit for $5.97 that includes a paint-roller tray, roller handle, two one-coat roller covers, a two-inch paint brush, a nine-by-twelve drop cloth, and a sixteen-inch extension pole that allows people to paint higher areas. Attention to such details makes people feel like the company cares enough about its customers to enable them to do the job—the whole job.

Taking the extra step to provide an unexpected service is just as worthwhile. For example, customers of Whole Foods Market in Palo Alto, California, can get on-the-spot massages inside the store. They pay $24 for thirty minutes of massage therapy, and no appointment is necessary.

Therapist Astrid K. Heinonen started offering massages inside the market to promote preventive health care in a place "where people would come every day and not expect stress relief." According to Heinonen, the service heightens Whole Foods' image. "They provide a healthy environment with good choices," she says.

Heinonen and the other massage therapists who work there are paid only by customers and not by Whole Foods. They use the space for a nominal charge and offer Whole Foods' employees a 50 percent discount.* Heinonen and the other massage therapists built their clientele by handing out business cards and offering private sessions.

Heinonen believes that the massage therapy has brought hundreds of new customers to the market: "A lot of people come in because of the massage, and then they shop. At least 50 percent of my clients say, 'This massage service is why I'm here.'"

Atone for Your Sins

In basketball when your opponent has a temporary numerical advantage—for example, a four-on-three fast break—it should score a basket against you. However, if your team steals the ball and then quickly scores a basket, it's called a four-point play because you not only prevented your opponent from scoring two points, you scored two points yourself.

Business four-point plays occur when a company fixes a mistake and wins back a customer who is about to leave or has already been lost. As in basketball, a four-point play is perturbing to the competition because it represents both an opportunity lost and an opponent's recovery.

While it's better not to lose a customer, it's also unrealistic to think it will never happen. I've lost some customers and got many (but not all) of them back. I've also been a lost customer and observed what companies have done to get me back. Here's how to atone for your sins:

▪ Take the Initiative

People prefer to hear the bad news as soon as they can. However, companies sit on bad news—thinking in some brain-dead way that customers won't notice or won't care, or that the problem will go away. For example, if your plane isn't at the gate thirty minutes† before a scheduled departure, you can pretty much be sure it won't be on time. Yet many airlines break the bad news to you after the scheduled departure time and annoy a bunch of already anxious flyers. So as soon as you know

---

*Giving employees a meaningful discount is an excellent way to recruit evangelists. (See Chapter 7.)
†Fifteen minutes if you're flying on Southwest Airlines.

your shipment is going to be late, there's a bug in your computer chip, or you can't fulfill a commitment, take the initiative and tell your customers before they have to ask.

▪ Be Honest

Bad news is bad news, so lying about the cause doesn't make it any better, and people hate being lied to. Once when I was flying to San Francisco, my plane was diverted to Sacramento because of fog in San Francisco, according to the pilot. After a one-hour delay in Sacramento, we flew to San Francisco where the sky was clear and the airport was operating without any delays. The bad news was that we would be arriving late, but lying about the reason pushed me over the top.

▪ Put the Customer in Control

When you screw up, the best person to choose the corrective action is the customer. Shouting that it's your company's policy to do such and such until the veins pop out of your forehead does no one any good. Instead, put the customer in control and ask him how he would like the problem fixed. Most people will be reasonable—indeed, partially because they feel like they are in control. Remember: company policies are overhead, customers are profit.

▪ Take Responsibility

In any transaction there are only two parties: one that pays and one that gets paid. Taking responsibility means that if you're the one that gets paid, you take full responsibility for problems, and you don't point the finger. For example, if a customer buys a car from you and the radio breaks, don't blame the radio manufacturer—just fix the radio. A corollary of this principle is that any employee should take responsibility for the actions of the entire company and not blame another department or employee.

Ironically, a customer who has been wronged can turn out to be your greatest supporter—even more so than a customer who has never tested your resolve—if you observe these principles. This is not to suggest that you should create bad situations on purpose, but every customer interaction, even if it starts off as a problem, is an opportunity.

Exercise

Call your company and claim that its product was defective or its service was unacceptable. Go through the process of trying to rectify the situation as your customer would. Does your company win you back?

Speak Well of the Living

No matter how much you focus on your existing and potential customers, some of them will ask questions like, "What do you think of X?" X being the company that's trying to do you in.

This is the only place in this book where I advocate an underhanded deed: Lie. That is, don't discuss your true feelings. Instead sugarcoat and caramelize your response: "X is a very fine company that we respect a great deal." Lay it on with a trowel, as Shakespeare would say.

In fact, the more positive your response the better. Come to praise Caesar *and* to bury him, as Shakespeare would not say. Then people will understand what you're really doing. Be careful, however, to describe your competition in absolute terms like good, fine, and excellent. Don't use relativistic statements like "X is better than we are." Some people may believe you.

Am I trying to turn you into a wimp? Not at all. There's little reason to provide kindling for your competition's ire unless it's your plan to enrage your competition so that it lashes out wildly and commits a blunder (and I would try to talk you out of this kind of strategy). Focus on your customer, lull your competition to sleep, and slay it in its slumber.

Let Bygones Be Bygones

Returning to our earlier literary example of one competitor driving another crazy, Captain Ahab could have focused on his customers, filling the need for oil by harpooning whales. Instead, he dedicated himself to killing Moby Dick, and we all know that Moby Dick proved to be the better competitor. Moby Dick may have symbolized evil, but Captain Ahab's obsession was its own kind of evil.

There are three business lessons to be gained from studying Captain Ahab: a) put your customers first; b) revenge is a lousy reason for fighting your enemies, so allow your brain to overrule your vengeful instinct; c) never fight a whale. Now, like Captain Ahab, you've been warned.

Interview: Jim Olson

I cannot think of a better example of a company that drives its competition crazy by focusing on its customers than Hewlett-Packard. This $25 billion company sells a vast range of products, including measurement and test instruments, calculators, computers, plotters, and laser printers.

High-technology companies like Hewlett-Packard sometimes lose sight of their customers' needs when they fall in love with technology: "If we invent it, they will come," they mistakenly tell themselves. Sometimes they will even continue to make a pet product after the market has passed them by.

Jim Olson, general manager of Hewlett-Packard's Video Communications Division, avoided this self-infatuation trap. In 1992 most of the Video Communications Division's current employees were designing microwave instruments. Sensing that this market had slowed, the company gutted the microwave division and created the Video Communications Division to find and satisfy unfulfilled needs.

The market that Hewlett-Packard found was video production and postproduction, and in a matter of months, its microwave engineers learned what the Hollywood and video crowd needed. The division's first products included test equipment for television studios, a video

70

server that stores and forwards video footage to end users, and a plain-paper video printer.

Q: How did your division make the transition from microwave to multimedia products?

Initially it was thought the direction wouldn't be all that different from where we were. We considered taking microwave technology and applying it to video-test problems. I came on board, hired a bunch of people, and we started looking at the multimedia marketplace.

We had an agreement with our corporate management that we would go from making money to losing a lot of money for a while, so we took our current R & D and marketing engineers and essentially we bought them airline tickets and sent them to attend trade shows and to meet customers.

Customers didn't care that we were from the microwave part of H-P. Studio customers said, "You're a great printer company. I'm in the video business. I'd love to own a printer that captured video images and put them on plain paper."

We used to jokingly refer to ourselves as gearhead engineers. The division was successful for a long time because we sold to other gearheads. Now we were going to be selling to people with ponytails and earrings—and those were the men. This is where putting the customer first really paid off because we went into these customer visits naive and ignorant.

We told people we didn't know anything about the industry, but that we thought we had a lot to offer. We listened better than if we went and talked to other microwave engineers. We went in not having personal relationships or detailed knowledge of customer behaviors and ended up really recognizing the buying habits of people.

One of the ways to drive your competition crazy is to succeed at seeing the forest from the trees, and we could do that because we had never been in this forest before.

Q: So ignorance was empowering?

Ignorance was incredibly empowering. I think our ability to succeed in the long term will depend on always pretending some bit of ignorance when talking with customers. There's no way anyone could do what we did without taking a fresh viewpoint of how to talk to customers, how to listen to them, and how to take what they tell you and go back and execute.

When you know an industry really well, you tend to impose your thinking on the customer. It's a little more confusing when you're struggling and don't know whether what you're doing is right or not. We clearly knew nothing and that really helped.

Q: What else did you learn in the process?

The first lesson is to clear your plate and make a commitment. Trying to ask a division to investigate a huge new business opportunity by investing just a little bit of resources is a ticket to failure.

I'm often asked why we didn't go out and hire a bunch of video people. Frankly, it would have been too slow. It would have taken a lot of time to recruit them, to train them, and to build an entity that operated the H-P way.

The second lesson is to resist management fads. For example, applying the same total quality management (TQM) methodology to every business, whether it's a start-up, turnaround, or growth-and-cash generator, is stupid. I'm a process kind of person and tried to use TQM, but we found it inadequate to meet the time-to-market requirements of a start-up.

The third lesson is to put your first-string players on the field. Every football team does this, but businesspeople are terrible at it. I went out looking for the cream of the crop, and we've done that at every level in the division, so now there's no tolerance at all here for poor performance.

Q: How has your competition reacted?

There are some things traded between competing engineers and managers at trade shows. We had a competitor come up to us at the recent NAB [National Association of Broadcasters] show and say, "Since you guys came to last year's NAB, you've made my life miserable. My boss is all over our asses to be like you guys and take a fresh view of the market."

Notes

[1]Kenichi Ohmae, "Getting Back to Strategy," *Harvard Business Review*, November-December 1988, 154.

[2]James Borghesani, "Blue Cross Goes to the Mall to Reach Customers," *Boston Business Journal*, 11 March 1994, 6.

[3]Michele Moreno, "Innovative Banker Uses the Personal Touch to Attract New Business," *On Achieving Excellence*, October 1992, 9.

[4]Valerie Reitman, "Toyota Calling," *Wall Street Journal*, 28 September 1994, 1.

Chapter 6

Concentrate on a Decisive Point

The principles of war could, for brevity, be condensed into a single word—'Concentration.'

Basil Liddell Hart

Divide and Conquer

In 1796 Napoleon was twenty-seven years old with no previous experience leading an army. Yet he became the commander in chief of the French army in Italy, where his first campaign was the Battle of Montenotte.

In this battle, Napoleon had thirty-five thousand troops, and his opponents, united against him, were an Austrian army of thirty-five thousand men and a Sardinian army of twenty-five thousand men. Napoleon ordered his forces to attack neither the Austrians nor the Sardinians. Instead he aimed for the point where the two armies were joined in order to drive a wedge between them.

When he secured this weak point, he turned his forces against the Sardinians, who surrendered. After three days of intense fighting, he defeated the Austrians, too.[1] Napoleon achieved success in this battle because he concentrated on a decisive point—a lesson that has proven applicable in business warfare as well. Divide and conquer makes perfect sense:

- It enables you to avoid overextension of your resources. Attacking a deeper-pocketed company over a broad range of products or markets is always risky.

- It minimizes or avoids retaliation. When you attack an isolated and seemingly unimportant area, your competitor may not even notice your attack. Or, it may not consider the area worth defending.

- It provides a small victory* to temper your troops and build their confidence for future battles. It can also attract customers and supporters and intimidate competitors.

Niche Thyself

I f Napoleon were a marketer, his action would be described as finding a niche and using it to bust open a market. A niche is a part of the market (or battlefield) that is well-suited to your capabilities—as the saying goes, "In the valley of the blind, the one-eyed man is king."

The Process

Finding a niche requires your having a great deal of knowledge about your own competitive advantages and the capabilities and attitudes of your competition. Armed with sufficient knowledge in these areas, you can usually detect niches using this four-step process:†

*Green Berets call this a "confidence target."
†The basis of this process is a discussion of Feature/Advantage/Benefit Grid and Feature Spectrum in *The Marketer's Visual Tool Kit* (New York: American Management Association, 1994, 47–51) by Terry Richey.

Step 1: Determine the most important features of your products or services and your competition's products or services. Be sure to include "soft" features such as service, support, and warranty coverage.

Step 2: Create a graph that looks like this:

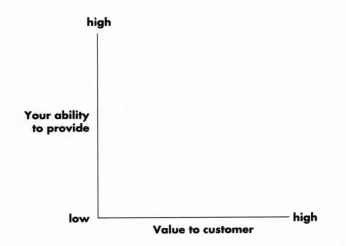

Step 3: Position all the features on the graph according to the parameters of your ability to provide the features and their value to the customer.

Step 4: Look for features that are high and to the right—that is, those that you can uniquely provide and are of high value to the customer. There's your niche.

Real-World Example

Here's how one company found a niche for itself and turned the location of emergency care into a decisive point.

Dr. Gresham Bayne of San Diego, California, discovered that 82 percent of emergency cases didn't require an ambulance ride or emergency-room services. The waste of medical resources put an onerous burden on both patient and hospital. Since most patients didn't need an ambulance and immediate attention at a fully outfitted emergency room, an entrepreneur like Bayne could disrupt the medical marketplace by concentrating on one point: the location of medical service.

Dr. Bayne purchased an ambulance and fitted it with a portable X-ray machine, a minilab, an EKG machine, and other supplies. He rode the ambulance to people's homes to make acute-care house calls. Based on his initial success, he formed a company called Call Doctor, Inc. Call Doctor has expanded to fifteen sites nationwide and also franchises its mobile emergency-room service.

Call Doctor medical technicians determine the seriousness of a case by asking a series of questions over the phone. For serious cases, a doctor is sent to a patient's home where he or she administers tests. The doctor can make further diagnoses or send the patient to the hospital if necessary. Some ambulances even contain mini-pharmacies to fill prescriptions on the spot.

The average charge for Call Doctor, $200, is nearly 70 percent less than the basic charge at emergency rooms in the San Diego area. The savings are even greater when the cost of the ambulance service is factored in.

Call Doctor concentrated on the *location* of medical care and turned it into a way to *serve* customers better. A diagram of Call Doctor's market using the niche-analysis process of the previous section would look like this:

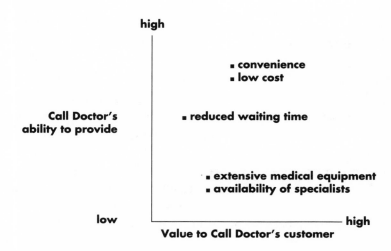

Call Doctor's service is high and to the right: providing convenience, low costs, and reduced waiting time. Most hospitals probably don't know Call

Doctor even exists, but someday the company may drive its competition crazy with a new way of providing low-cost, convenient medical care. Or it may force the competition to do the same.

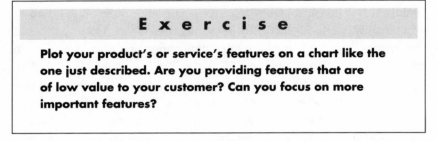

E x e r c i s e

Plot your product's or service's features on a chart like the one just described. Are you providing features that are of low value to your customer? Can you focus on more important features?

Cover the Earth

A niche is a nice place for a while. But other companies are usually beckoned by an attractive niche and will eventually ruin the neighborhood. Also, the one-eyed man may be king in the valley of the blind, but there aren't that many valleys of blind people. Daring companies cover the earth: they attack, consolidate, and then attack again.

The Honda Example

A dramatic example of a cover-the-earth strategy is Honda's entry into the U.S. car market. The first Honda products in America were inexpensive motorcycles. In a sense, Honda concentrated on a point that didn't *exist* as far as American car manufacturers were concerned, since they didn't sell motorcycles.

From cheap motorcycles, Honda progressed to higher-end motorcycles. Still no car manufacturer noticed Honda. Then Honda brought in tiny, low-end automobiles like the Civic. These early cars were little more than motorcycles with bodies—especially in the opinion of Ford, General Motors, or Chrysler.

Then Honda started producing upscale cars like the Accord. By this time American car manufacturers began to notice Honda, but it was too

The N600: the first car Honda sold in America.

late. Consumers had come to identify Honda with inexpensive, well-made cars. Finally, Honda introduced a luxury car marque called Acura, which included a world-class sports car called the NSX.

The Law of Increasing Returns

Tne powerful technique for covering the earth is called the Law of Increasing Returns. This concept holds that the more people who use your product, the more likely it is that a potential customer can talk to someone who already owns your product, and—assuming your product is satisfactory—be influenced to buy your product.

The Law of Increasing Returns explains many business success stories—for example, Toyota's introduction of the Lexus marque in 1989. A Lexus was a high-quality car that rivaled a Mercedes or BMW at about half the cost.

Because it cost less than other luxury cars, more people could afford one. Because so many people bought one, it became easy to talk to someone who owned one. Because the opinion of these people was good, more people bought a Lexus, and the cycle was repeated.

Sometimes the Law of Increasing Returns explains the success of products that should not have remained successful. For example, typewriters and computers use a QWERTY keyboard which was originally designed in 1873 to limit typing speed because mechanical typewriters could not keep up with fast typists. (The name QWERTY comes from the six letters in a row on the left side of the keyboard.)

In 1888 a competition was staged between QWERTY typist Frank E. McGurrin and non-QWERTY typist Louis Taub. McGurrin trounced Taub, and the widespread interpretation was that the QWERTY keyboard was a superior design. This competition was a crucial event that added to the momentum of the QWERTY keyboard.[2]

Decades later, computers do not use keys to strike paper so alternate layouts could enable faster typing, but the first computer manufacturers copied the QWERTY design anyway. More efficient keyboards, such as the Dvorak Simplified Keyboard (DSK), would enable millions of computer users to enter text more quickly.

The Law of Increasing Returns worked against progress: people were already using the QWERTY keyboard, so early computer manufacturers adopted it for their keyboards, so more people used it, so more computer manufacturers copied it, and now we're stuck with it.[3] (The U.S. Navy, ever mindful of efficiency, found that the increased speed of DSK would amortize the cost of retraining typists within ten days of full employment.[4])

The point is that the more people who use your product, the better it will be for you because there will be more word-of-mouth hubbub. Thus, the ramifications of the Law of Increasing Returns are:

- Samples are important. The best advertising is people who are familiar with your product, so use some of those advertising dollars for samples. The use of samples is obvious in product-oriented businesses, but those of you in service businesses can offer to do small projects or partial analysis and accomplish the same result.
(Be sure to read John Spencer's interview in the next chapter about providing samples of Glide dental floss.)

- It's better to sow than to skim. Introducing your product at a lower, more affordable price encourages trial and therefore builds a larger installed base. The more customers out there intially, the better, so sow now and skim later.

- Beware (or exploit) the critical event. The face-off between McGurrin and Taub, in hindsight, legitimized the QWERTY keyboard. Nobody remembers that this was only one contest, and that Taub was a hunt-and-peck typist who used four fingers on a keyboard without shift keys so that upper- and lowercase letters had separate keys.

- Get to market quickly—and not just because of marketing paranoia. This is not to say that you should ship an inferior product, but the clock is ticking, and you have a finite amount of time to establish a standard. Show this paragraph to your engineers who are trying to get you to let them add "just one more feature."

- The best product may not necessarily win. The first *acceptable* product or the fast-second product with good marketing may win. For example, the Windows operating system for personal computers outsells Macintosh despite its later entry and inferiority.

E x e r c i s e

How difficult is it for potential customers to talk to existing customers about your products or services? Are there ways to make this easier?

Provide an Alternative

As the cartoon character Pogo once said, "We have met the enemy, and he is us." Sometimes you become your own worst enemy when your strategy is to emulate the leader in your marketplace. Unfortunately, it's difficult to unseat a leader with a frontal assault, so if you're the number two (or lower) company, your decisive point of attack is often dictated by a simple principle: Provide an alternative to the leader.

Al Ries and Jack Trout, the authors of *The 22 Immutable Laws of Marketing*, call this The Law of the Opposite. According to Ries and Trout, "If you want to establish a firm foothold on the second rung of the ladder, study the firm above you. Where is it strong? And how do you turn that strength into a weakness?"[5]

Here are some examples of how companies have provided an alternative to the leader and tried to drive it crazy:

- Pepsi versus Coke. Coke is an old, established product. Pepsi is for the "new generation." *If you're stodgy, drink Coke. If you're hip, drink Pepsi.*

- Burger King versus McDonald's. McDonald's is for kids. Burger King is for people who have grown up. *If you're a juvenile, eat at McDonald's. If you're an adult, eat at Burger King.*

- DHL versus Federal Express. Federal Express is terrific for shipping small packages *within* the United States. DHL covers the rest of the world. *If you have a shipment within the United States, use Federal Express. If you have a shipment anywhere else, use DHL.*

In each of these examples, the number two company shouldn't try to emulate the leader: Pepsi can't out-"establish" Coke, Burger King can't appeal more to kids than McDonald's, and DHL can't usurp the overnight shipping business in the United States. These companies conceded the strong point of the leader, put a spin on it to turn it into a vulnerability, and offered their own goods or services as the more attractive alternative.

Exercise

How could you provide an alternative to these industry leaders?

a. **Hertz**

b. **Nike**

c. **Microsoft**

d. **United Airlines**

Make Value, Not War

And we will all go together when we go,
What a comforting fact that is to know.
Universal bereavement,
An inspiring achievement,
Yes, we all will go together when we go.[6]

You may be wondering why one of the recommendations of this chapter isn't to concentrate on the decisive point of pricing. Traditional thinking goes like this: "Market share is the key to profitability, and lower prices increase market share, so let's start a price war to drive our competition crazy and get rich."

Such thinking has led to disastrous price wars for the airline, cigarette, accounting, and computer memory industries. The reason is simple: Correlation does not equal causation. Market share and profitability may be correlated, but this doesn't mean that market share *caused* profitability. When people misperceive market share as the cause of profitability, then they are tempted to use an inappropriate weapon like pricing to achieve profitability. In business *post hoc, ergo propter hoc** is usually untrue. "After this, therefore *despite* this" is more likely.

Exercise

If you noticed that the executives of successful companies drove expensive cars, would you buy expensive cars for your managers to make your company successful?

Let me try to talk you out of using pricing as a primary weapon against your competition. My source for this section is an exceptional book called *The Strategy and Tactics of Pricing* by Thomas Nagle and Reed Holden.† According to Nagle and Holden, "Pricing is like playing chess. Those who make moves one at a time—seeking to minimize immedi-

*More Latin: After this, therefore because of this.
†Run, do not walk, to your favorite bookstore and buy this book.

83

ate losses or to exploit immediate opportunities—will invariably be beaten by those who can envision the game a few moves ahead."[7]

Most companies only consider pricing decisions in a closed, static space. Simplistically—very simplistically—companies think that if they lower prices, they will get more customers. Their plan for waging and winning a price war considers only themselves and customers:

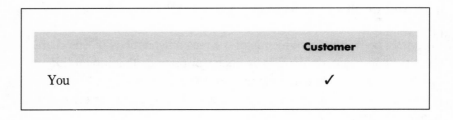

	Customer
You	✓

However, this approach doesn't take into account the reactions of competitors who may match reductions, surpass reductions, hold steady, increase prices, or increase value (for example, by bundling additional services). Thus, plans for a price war should include other companies:

	Customer
You	✓
Competitor A	✓
Competitor B	✓
Competitor C	✓

The chart is still incomplete, however, because "the customer" is usually a heterogeneous collection of diverse groups with different needs. This diversity should likewise be considered for pricing decisions:

	Customer A	Customer B	Customer C	Customer D
You	✓		✓	
Competitor A	✓		✓	✓
Competitor B	✓	✓		✓
Competitor C	✓		✓	
Competitor D	✓	✓	✓	

Then there is the element of time—or rounds. That is, in the first round, you may lower prices and customer A may buy more, but competitor A may lower prices to match your move. In the second round, you may lower prices again and competitor B may join the fray—and so on. Get the picture? Before you declare a price war, you had better consider all the ramifications of the actions and reactions of your competition and your customers *over time*.

Price "war" is an appropriate metaphor because in war both sides usually lose if the conflict lasts long enough. Price "diplomacy" is a better metaphor to aspire to. Diplomacy involves minimizing the frequency and ferocity of war by sending signals to enemies and increasing the non-price appeal of your products and services. Here are some ways to do so:

- Communicate a willingness and ability to retaliate. Chrysler once told the business press that it had a low-cost minivan design that it would manufacture if it had to. Essentially, Chrysler was telling other manufacturers not to start a minivan price war because it was willing and able to win this war.

E x e r c i s e

Airlines used to signal one another that their airfare changes were retaliatory by beginning the price code change with an "FU."[8] What do you think FU stood for?

a. **Fouled Up**

b. **Feeling Uppity**

c. **Forever Unprofitable**

d. **Finally Unmeetable**

e. **Firmly Unrealistic**

■ Create an umbrella for your competition. For example, if you raise your prices in one segment and simultaneously increase the value of your products or services in another, you may find that your competition is attracted by the umbrella of your high prices in the former and avoids competing in the latter. In this way, it's possible to divide up the market and coexist.

■ Fire warning shots. Suppose a competitor goes to your best customers and selectively undercuts your price to gain their business. Rather than declaring war, go to your competitor's best customers and mention the lowball prices they were "probably" paying. Of course, these customers are probably not paying the lowball prices, so they complain to your competitor, and your competitor will get the message.

■ Increase the value of your product or service. Rather than lowering your price, improve your product or service by increasing the warranty length, improving technical support, guaranteeing delivery, eliminating shipping costs, or providing free or inexpensive upgrades. Premier Industrial Corporation, for example, performs a computer analysis of its customer's used engine oil to assist them in identifying engine problems.

Are there any times when it pays to use pricing as a way to drive your competition crazy? Yes, under very specific conditions such as these:

- You have a sustainable, unique, and significant cost differential. Perhaps you've invented (and patented!) a new manufacturing process.*

- You can use a low price to hook customers and then sell them add-on or supplemental products or services that are more profitable. Microsoft, for example, can give away the Windows operating system in order to sell more application software.

- Your products or services appeal to small segments and you're competing with a behemoth who cannot afford to meet your price challenge. For example, you operate a local delivery service, and you undercut national delivery services who can't lower prices in your area without lowering prices everywhere.

In most cases, however, my recommendation is to make value, not war. A price war is simply too dangerous, and I don't know any company that went broke creating too much value for its customers. Or, as Nagle and Holden say, "... the goal of a strategic plan should not be to become bigger than the competition (although that may happen), but to become *better* [emphasis theirs]."[9]

Strive for Constant Disruption

One danger of concentrating on a decisive point is that your competition can get so much insight from your actions that it can turn its blindness and weakness into strengths. Honda, for example, bludgeoned General Motors and other American manufacturers into creating their own versions of economical, high-quality cars.

There isn't a way to avoid this danger, but you can minimize its effects by disrupting the marketplace as a continuing *process*, not a sole

*But then again, since you're not after market share for the sake of market share, why not just make more money?

event. If your competition is worthy, it will fix, improve, and debug its own weaknesses—negating your advantages. So you must disrupt the marketplace again and again.

Unfortunately, disrupting the marketplace the second time around may be harder. According to Gary Hamel and C. K. Prahalad, the authors of *Competing for the Future*, "To be a challenger once, it is enough to challenge the orthodoxies of the incumbents; to be a challenger twice, a firm must be capable of challenging its own orthodoxies."[10]

Winning and losing are both temporary states that can quickly change. If you're on top, your competition may be catching up. If you're on the bottom, you can disrupt the marketplace and emerge on top. In both cases you must constantly disrupt the marketplace or turn into a laggard.

The bottom line is: Attack a decisive point, branch out, and strive for constant disruption.

Notes

[1] David Rogers, *Waging Business Warfare* (New York: Kensington Publishing Corp., 1987), 146–48.

[2] Stephen Jay Gould, *Bully for Brontosaurus: Reflections in Natural History* (New York: W. W. Norton & Company, 1991), 70–71.

[3] M. Mitchell Waldrop, *Complexity* (New York: Simon & Schuster, 1992), 35.

[4] Ibid., 63.

[5] Al Ries and Jack Trout, *The 22 Immutable Laws of Marketing* (New York: HarperBusiness, 1993), 51.

[6] Tom Lehrer, *We Will All Go Together When We Go* (1958)

[7] Thomas Nagle and Reed Holden, *The Strategy and Tactics of Pricing*, 2d ed. (Englewood Cliffs, N.J.: Prentice Hall, 1995), 115–40.

[8] Asra Nomani, "Airlines May Be Using a Price Data Network to Lessen Competition," *Wall Street Journal*, 28 June 1990, A6.

[9] Thomas Nagle and Reed Holden, *The Strategy and Tactics of Pricing*, 2d ed. (Englewood Cliffs, N.J.: Prentice Hall, 1995), 115–40.

[10] Gary Hamel and C. K. Prahalad, *Competing for the Future* (Boston: Harvard Business School Press, 1994), 61.

Chapter 7

Turn Customers into Evangelists

One person with a belief is equal to a force of ninety-nine who only have interest.

John Stuart Mill

Raging, Inexorable Macintosh Thunderlizards

When Apple introduced Macintosh in January 1984, most of the experts in the computer industry thought that it was a neat computer that was doomed to fail because it did not support the industry-standard MS-DOS operating system.

From their point of view, we were trying to sell a computer without software that was manufactured by a flaky company of ex-hippies led by an East Coast executive who had sold sugar water for his father-in-law. (To a large degree, this was an accurate assessment.)*

What the naysayers did not foresee was that Apple could muster a cadre of raging, inexorable thunderlizard evangelists who could buoy Macintosh by providing emotional and technical support when Apple itself was unable or unwilling to do so.

These early adopters fell in love with Macintosh when it didn't have software and ran too slow. Anyone can commit to a perfect machine—these people had real courage. They demonstrated Macintosh to prospective users. They undermined corporate computer standards and smuggled Macintosh into companies that had standardized on IBM products—to the consternation of raging, inexplicable IBM blunder bigots.

They made IBM's mountain into a molehill and counteracted IBM's larger size, solid image, and installed base. IBM may have had *legitimacy*, but we had *passion*. Let no one tell you differently: evangelism is the reason Macintosh became a successful product.

This chapter explains how to turn your customers into raging, inexorable thunderlizards for your product, service, company, or idea.

Create a Cause

The starting point for evangelism is a cause—something you believe in and want others to believe in as much as you do. It can be a product like Macintosh, a company like Saturn, or a set of beliefs like a cleaner environment.

Creating a good product or service is the first step in turning your customers into evangelists. (This explains why so few companies have evangelists—that is, because so few companies have great products or services.) You can create products and services in three ways:

- Method 1: Ask customers what they want. Result: Me-too products that perpetually trail the products of the leaders of your industry.

- Method 2: Manipulate customers to buy what you sell. Result: The ill will of the marketplace as people realize they've been had.

*Respectively, Steve Jobs and Steve Wozniak, John Sculley, Pepsi-Cola, and Donald Kendall, the chairman and CEO of PepsiCo at the time.

■ Method 3: Combine insight into the potential of innovation, a love of what you're doing, and an understanding of needs (both mature and newborn). Result: A cause.

Few people want to be associated with a mediocre product or a manipulative company—let alone get excited about them—so I recommend the third method. (For more insight into creating a cause, read *If You Want to Write* by Brenda Ueland. It is the best book ever written about product development.)

If you successfully create a cause, you'll see that a cause is set apart from everyday products and services in these ways:

■ A cause embodies a vision. A cause isn't a namby-pamby, me-too idea. It is a radically different way to radically change the world— or at least make a dent in the world. It represents someone's dream. It is a calling, not just a good idea.

■ A cause seizes the high ground. It isn't negative, destructive, or neutral. Its intent is to make the world better whether by making people more productive, cleaning up the environment, or empowering disenfranchised groups, to give a few examples.

Exercise

Think of a moral high ground for a company in the following industries:

a. **Athletic shoes**

b. **Family restaurants**

c. **Personal computers**

d. **Camera equipment**

■ A cause redefines experiences. It creates new needs, sets standards for industries or marketplaces, and changes how things are done. A cause has effects that are irreversible. The Body Shop, for example, is a cause that has changed how hair-care and skin-care products are sold throughout the world.

- A cause catalyzes strong feelings. A cause polarizes people into groups who love them and hate them. Everyday products and services are barely worth thinking about and do not arouse strong emotions. People *want* a vision. People *accept* a me-too idea.

Find the Right People

When we introduced Macintosh, we focused on selling Macintoshes to the presidents, vice presidents, and directors of large companies. This was the wrong approach, and it taught us a valuable lesson: Find the *right* people to carry your torch, not necessarily the people with the right title.

We thought that the titles had the power, and they could enforce a top-down decision to purchase Macintoshes. But the titles were far removed from the actual use of computers, so explaining Macintosh to them was like trying to explain clouds to a fish. Furthermore, the titles weren't going to force changes in corporate computer standards—they had created these standards, so changing them now would be admitting a mistake.

E x e r c i s e

Call your company and identify yourself with an impressive title. Then call your company and identify yourself without an impressive title. Does treatment differ?

Instead, the grass roots made Macintosh successful: artists, designers, secretaries, temps, summer students, and interns. Luckily, we learned this quickly and shifted our attention to the right people. (With hindsight, we could have learned this earlier by contemplating the methods of the greatest salesman who ever lived, Jesus. Instead of targeting high holies and Pharisees, he pursued tax collectors, prostitutes, and fishermen— that is, picking the people who could commit to his cause.)

In the process of finding the people who could commit to Macintosh, we learned the following lessons about evangelizing a cause:

■ *Pursue the existing customers of your company.* Since you already have a relationship with these people, it's easier to ratchet them up to higher levels of commitment. My experience is that the best evangelists come out of your customer base.

■ *Don't be afraid to ask for help.* People like to help a company with a great product or service. They want to be associated with a winner. They will be flattered, not offended, by your requests.

■ *Let people help any way they can.* Some people may want to demonstrate your product. Others may want to write about it in their community newsletter. Let a thousand flowers bloom because you never know which zany idea will be the one that makes you the most money or saves your company.

■ *Ignore a person's background.* A good evangelist only needs to love your product and be willing to spread the good news. Furthermore, a person with impressive educational credentials and work experience is often the least likely to want to adopt a new product or company.

The bottom line is this: Ignore people's titles and look for people who "get it." They may or may not have executive positions, but that's not the point. You want people who understand your cause, are enthusiastic about it, and want to help you.

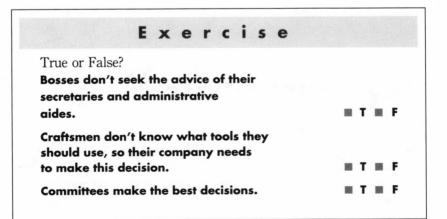

Exercise

True or False?
Bosses don't seek the advice of their secretaries and administrative aides.   ■ T ■ F

Craftsmen don't know what tools they should use, so their company needs to make this decision.   ■ T ■ F

Committees make the best decisions.   ■ T ■ F

Let People Test-Drive Your Product

How do you determine if people understand and like your cause? The answer is to let them test drive or touch your cause and decide for themselves. The philosophical underpinning is that you believe your customers are smart, and if you give them information, they can draw their own conclusions.

Manufacturers of products like shampoo, skin lotion, and foods frequently provide samples. Hear Music, a music-store chain with outlets in Santa Monica, Berkeley, and Palo Alto, pushes the envelope of test driving by enabling customers to sample hundreds of compact discs. Although many music stores allow you to listen to a compact disc before buying it, there are usually only a handful of listening stations in the store. Hear Music has about forty.

Customers can walk up to a particular section (say, Latin Jazz), put on headphones, look over the display of ten compact discs set up, and push the play-button underneath the compact disc they want to hear. If customers want to hear a compact disc that isn't already set up for sampling, they can take it to the front, and the "DJ" will take off the shrink-wrap and play it for them at a listening bar with headsets.

Hear Music's setup compels people to put on the headphones—and therefore buy more compact discs than they intended. The store is so well designed that you *want* to buy something. Thus, by enabling people to test drive compact discs before they buy them, Hear Music is creating evangelists not only for its stores but also for recording artists.

Provide an Easy First Step

Once you've found potential evangelists, the next action is to give your prospects an easy and safe first step. This means you should avoid forcing them into making a commitment to your cause that threatens their career, jeopardizes their prestige, or risks a large amount of money.

Here are some examples of easy and hard first steps to illustrate the difference:

Cause/Business	Easy First Step	Hard First Step
Environmentalism	Recycle cans, bottles, and newspapers at home	Donate $10,000 and picket Congress
Personal computer company	Create newsletters	Throw out all existing computers and establish a new corporate standard
Marketing consultant	Manage the introduction of a small product	Write the company's five-year strategic plan
Hair salon	Shampoo and condition	Dye and cut
Airplane manufacturer	Take a flying lesson	Buy a plane
Graphic designer	Design a flyer or product fact sheet	Revamp all collateral and point-of-purchase material

The goal is to give budding evangelists a safe, smooth, and nonthreatening way to join your cause. Enlisting should be like walking up a gentle slope where, after a short time, evangelists can look back and see that they're at the top of a hill.

Make Customers Feel Like Part of Your Team

The last step in turning your customers into evangelists is to make people feel as if they are part of your team. On a practical level, they *are* part of your team—they're just not paid. So why would they join?

First, there's the personal satisfaction of helping others discover a good product. Second, there's the prestige of knowing that you found something good before others did—you're an on-top-of-things-early adopter. Third, there's the attraction of belonging to a close-knit group.

Rykä Incorporated of Norwood, Massachusetts, makes aerobic instructors part of the product design team. The company was started from an end-user design perspective when its founder, Sheri Poe, could not find comfortable aerobics shoes. After weeks of searching, she concluded that women's athletic shoes were scaled-down versions of men's athletic shoes, despite the differences in female anatomy.

To continue the tradition of serving women's needs, Poe's company created the Rykä Training Body program. This program provides aerobics instructors discounts on Rykä shoes in exchange for design information and product feedback.

Laurie Ruddy, Rykä's director of marketing and strategic accounts, described how its work with instructors helps the company: "The program gets our product to key influencers who in turn get our name out there, create brand recognition, and get their students to wear them. By the mere fact that an instructor is wearing Rykä shoes, she will get questions from students and clients."

Thus, the members of the Training Body program serve as a direct line to and from Rykä's prospective customers: women in aerobics classes. There are more than twenty thousand instructors in the program, so Rykä maintains a large presence in their market at low expense.

People can also join your sales team. For example, Garden Way, the manufacturer of Troy-Bilt rototiller machines, refers sales prospects to a nearby volunteer who owns one of the company's products. The company recruits these volunteer salespeople to its "Good Neighbors" program at the time of purchase by offering them a discount or free attachment.

Troy-Bilt owners are cultish about their machines and like to spread the good news. Garden Way has both a dealership network and a "virtual" network of Troy-Bilt evangelists who fill in the gaps. These evangelists support the company by providing credible information to potential customers.[1]

Don't Forget Your Employees

Although the title of this chapter is "Turn Customers into Evangelists," don't forget to turn your employees into evangelists, too. All your employees should be evangelists—not just executives, salespeople, and marketers.

Every employee of Kiwi International, the airline based in Newark, New Jersey, attends a training class in which they're taught that all Kiwi employees are salespeople. Then they are encouraged (but receive no extra compensation) to visit travel agents in their hometowns to evangelize their airline.

Thus, as major airlines are cutting back their sales forces, Kiwi is expanding theirs. "We have nine hundred potential salespeople at Kiwi. A major airline might have five or six representatives in a major city. In the New York/New Jersey area alone we have five hundred people doing sales activity," states Beth Mack, vice president of sales and marketing for Kiwi.

According to Mack, travel agents appreciate being visited by Kiwi employees because they don't usually meet airline personnel face to face. The visit personalizes the company and goes a long way toward making people believe you're credible and real and that you appreciate them.

By contrast, in the summer of 1989, Eastern Airlines employees visited travel agencies not to evangelize them but to ask them not to sell Eastern flights because they were on strike. Eastern no longer exists.

E x e r c i s e

Are all your employees good enough to call on your customers?

Whether you're evangelizing employees or customers, find or create a great cause, find the right people, make them feel like part of your team, and go make history. You'll drive your competition crazy in the process.

Interview: John Spencer

John Spencer had his work cut out for him. He works for W. L. Gore & Associates of Newark, Delaware, the maker of Goretex, where he is the product champion for Glide dental floss. Spencer faced a difficult challenge in introducing Glide because Gore had an established name in fabrics and outdoor wear but not dental products.

Like the folks at Rykä, Spencer utilized professionals in a field to generate credible word-of-mouth (no pun intended) advertising for his product. As opposed to aerobics instructors, Spencer courted dentists in order to reach the ultimate consumer. In this interview, he explains how he created dental-floss evangelists.

Q: Why did you work with dental professionals to introduce Glide?

Early on we recognized that there were two markets: dental professionals and the ultimate consumer. We needed the pull-through of recommendations from dental professionals, so a year before selling our floss to retail, we began sending product samples to dentists and dental hygienists. Every dentist and dental hygienist in the country received a sample of floss.

These professionals were used to buying Johnson & Johnson, Oral-B, and Butler floss, so we sent an order form with significant discounts for professionals with every order and sample. We'd say in the mailing, "Requests to local stores to provide Glide would be appreciated." When the dentist got used to our floss, he or she would call a local store, and that store would call us, and we would sell directly to them.

If you're going in for the first time to a large retailer and they don't know your name you probably won't get in the door. By the time we got to stores, maybe the buyer had gotten a sample from his or her dentist. In general, it wasn't like we walked in completely cold.

Q: Were any of the dentists reluctant to accept samples?

They didn't have a choice—we bought lists from the American Dental Association and the American Dental Hygienists' Association, and we sent samples to all 225,000 dental professionals in the United States.

Q: Did the patients make the floss popular among dentists or vice versa?

The dentists and dental hygienists were the ones to be convinced first of the product's quality. They acted as salespeople to the patients.

Q: What prompted you to focus on giving out samples versus launching a traditional marketing campaign?

If you just tell people about Glide floss, they've heard it all before, so you won't have an effective program. But if people get a chance to try it, the differences are immediately obvious. Our entire marketing strategy when we first started in 1992—and even today—is aimed at getting product in someone's hands.

We do sampling at dental meetings and all the leading dental trade shows. We also do sampling with *Women's Sports & Fitness* magazine. Whenever the magazine's employees give away promotional bags to attendees of sports events, they include a sample of Glide floss. We also ran an ad in the March 1994 issue of *Architectural Digest*. The header says "Free," and the ad includes an 800 number for a free floss sample.

Q: Were you nervous about committing the resources necessary to reach so many people?

The key to starting any business is that you don't sample your prospects all at once. It took us six months to send samples to all 225,000 people. We started out with 4,000 and got initial feedback and information from those professionals.

Then we expanded our mailings in a controlled manner. We had to make sure we could manage the resources for filling incoming orders and that we could maintain our credibility during that time.

Q: What can you say to a small player entering a market of giants?

If you educate the consumer and request their assistance in educating others, people will ask for your product. Gore may be large in the fabrics industry, but in retail we had no presence at all.

A lot of people think you have to be a Procter & Gamble to be successful, but you can educate people about your product's benefits and availability if you have a product you believe in.

Note

[1] "Hands On: Sales & Marketing," *Inc.*, September 1991, 121.

Chapter 8

Make Good by Doing Good

Beautiful faces are they that wear
The light of a pleasant spirit there;
Beautiful hands are they that do
Deeds that are noble, good and true;
Beautiful feet are they that go
Swiftly to lighten another's woe.

McGuffey's Second Reader

The Art of Renting Cars

In 1994 Alamo Rent-A-Car sponsored an exhibit of eighty paintings called *American Impressionism and Realism: The Painting of Modern Life, 1885–1915*.[1] The exhibit was shown at New York's Metropolitan Museum of Art, and then moved to Fort Worth's Amon Carter Museum, the Denver Art Museum, and the Los Angeles County Museum of Art. It included works by John Singer Sargent, Mary Cassatt, and Robert Henri.

Alamo's exhibit received tremendous public exposure and garnered greater public awareness of Alamo as a big player in the car-rental business. It was part of an effort to disrupt the four-horse car-rental market made up of Hertz, Avis, National, and Budget, and it illustrates the principle of doing something good for society that also benefits your organization.

The promotional link between Alamo and the museums was masterful in its completeness:

- Coupons for discounts on car rentals were enclosed in the exhibition's educational brochures.

- People who bought something from the Metropolitan Museum's gift shop (including the museum's thirteen gift shops around the country) also received discount coupons.

- Opening-day attendees received a commemorative travel guide explaining how to get to the scenes in the exhibit.

- Travel guides were available to customers who rented Cadillacs in the regions that hosted the exhibit.

- The museum received 5 percent of the car-rental fees when coupon holders used Alamo.

In addition to these promotional links to increase short-term sales, sponsoring the event garnered Alamo three "fuzzy" benefits that were probably more important in the long run:

- The event expanded Alamo's image because most people associate sponsorship of this kind of event with large, successful blue-chip companies like General Electric and Hallmark.

- For a company in an industry known for cutthroat competition, the alliance with "the arts" enhanced Alamo's image as a company above the fray that had a sense of talent, taste, and creativity.

- Prior to the exhibit, people thought of Alamo as a company that rents vacation cars in vacation cities. Exposure in New York, Dallas/Ft. Worth, Denver, and Los Angeles increased awareness of Alamo's presence in the minds of business travelers.

Find a Sensible Tie-In

The Alamo example illustrates one way to increase sales and improve your image while you do something good for society. (What better way to drive your competition crazy?) This is a powerful technique that requires, as a first step, finding a tie-in between your company and a suitable philanthropic effort.

In Alamo's case, the company saw a link between renting cars to travelers as they fly around the United States and the scenes depicted in the art exhibits. The tie-in makes sense. By contrast, the tie-in between women's tennis (power, efficacy, and fitness) and Virginia Slims (a cigarette brand) no longer makes sense unless the cigarette company is advocating dependence on nicotine instead of men.

The Virginia Slims example illustrates that a tie-in must continue to make sense, so review the suitability of your programs from time to time. Initially the tie-in of women's tennis and women's liberation (as symbolized by the freedom to smoke in public) was acceptable. However, because of the danger of smoking, it no longer is.

E x e r c i s e

Think of a company that could create a sensible tie-in with the following philanthropic causes:

a. **Child abuse**

b. **Adult illiteracy**

c. **Homeless people**

d. **Lung cancer**

Hanna Andersson, the manufacturer of upscale clothes for children, provides an obvious example of a sensible tie-in. This Portland, Oregon–based company launched a program called Hannadowns in 1984. Customers can return used Hanna Andersson clothing and receive a 20 percent discount on future purchases.[2] The company has issued over $1.4 million in discounts and donated over 300,000 pieces of clothing.

Gun Denhart, the founder of the company, described her perspective on supporting social causes: "You can look at the problems of this society and say, 'Oh, too overwhelming, I can't do anything.' Or, you can say, 'I'll do a little bit, at least, to make this a better world.' "[3]

Hannadowns is powerful because it appeals on three different fronts: first, supporting a company that is socially responsible; second, recovering value out of clothes that can no longer be used; and third, receiving the 20 percent discount. These factors help consumers overcome spending guilt—transforming shopping into a socially responsible act.

A final example: Safeway and Apple Computer created a program where schools could collect Safeway receipts and then redeem these receipts for computer equipment from Apple. This promotion made sense because one of Apple's strongholds is the education market.

Everyone was a winner: schools obtained computer equipment they could not otherwise afford, Safeway created another reason for parents to shop at their supermarkets, and Apple got their computers into the hands of students who would, it hoped, tell their parents they needed an Apple computer and who would use an Apple computer for the rest of their lives.

Pick Something You Know

I n addition to finding a sensible tie-in, it's also wise to associate your company with an issue that you understand and care deeply about. Michael Egan, the chief executive officer and majority owner of Alamo, is a painter. This helped Alamo design its promotion with greater sensitivity to what would make it successful. Here are more examples.

- Valvoline Instant Oil Change, Inc., of Lexington, Kentucky, solicits used motor oil from do-it-yourselfers. One government estimate is that these do-it-yourselfers improperly dispose of 200 million gallons of used oil per year—about thirty times what was spilled out of the Exxon *Valdez*.

  According to Valvoline, employees feel good about preventing pollution, customers like to patronize a company that cares about the community's resources, and environmental groups can refer people to another kind of recycling center.[4]

■ Reebok International sponsors a program called P.E. TV that features famous athletes explaining techniques of their sport. The program is broadcast to junior-high and high-school students via Channel One, the commercial educational television channel. Reebok's program doesn't contain any advertising, but sponsorship entitles the company to show its name, logo, products, and athlete endorsers.

Reebok's total expenditures for the program are $2 million.* For this sum, Reebok builds brand awareness in a prime shoe-buying audience, and schools receive educational material for their students. In its brutal competition with Nike, Reebok is using alignment with a cause it truly knows—sports—as a potent weapon.[5]

■ Finally, a food market called Jim's Piggly Wiggly in Oshkosh, Wisconsin, takes picking something you know one step further by letting customers choose among the causes the market supports. Piggly Wiggly donates 1 percent of its sales to more than ninety nonprofit organizations. Customers select the cause they wish to support by delivering or sending their receipts to the charities. When the receipts total $2,500 in sales, Piggly Wiggly grants the charity $25.[6]

Build in a Feedback Mechanism

Warm and fuzzies aside, it's nice to know if your efforts are yielding tangible results as well as boosting your image. To get this information, try to devise a method to measure how successful your attempts to link doing good and doing business have been.

For example, by providing coupons to exhibit attendees and shoppers and measuring their redemption rate, Alamo could gauge the value of the exhibit as a means to promote their company as a car-rental provider.

Similarly, Hanna Andersson knows the amount of discounts that

---

*It probably costs Nike, Reebok's competition, that much to leave a voice-mail message for Michael Jordan.

have been used because of its Hannadowns program, and Apple knows how many schools bought Macintoshes by using Safeway purchases.

E x e r c i s e

If your effort to do something good for society didn't increase your business by a dollar, would you still do it?

Beware of the Pitfalls

The final topic is the downside of doing good to make good. This sequence of actions almost sounds too good to be true: you help people, improve your image, and garner exposure. It *is* too good to be entirely true, so beware of the pitfalls that face you:

- Don't create sales and promotional programs that reek of commercialization. Coupons in a brochure or shopping bag are okay. "Alamo" banners plastered on the front of an art museum are not, and Alamo was careful to avoid such crassness.

- If you live by philanthropy, you may die by philanthropy. You're in business to create profits. You can do this in a socially responsible way and even return some profits to society, but don't forget that you have to make money to survive. Mind the store, not just the rain forest.

- By linking doing good and doing business, you paint a bullseye on your back. Your socially responsible actions may not be enough for some and too much for others. You'll be held to higher standards than other companies. If you want the upside of free publicity, keep your house in order because few things delight the press more than exposing hypocrisy.

- Your efforts to do good and to align with issues may attract the

106

wrong kind of employee. It may also repel a job candidate you need. The overarching qualifications for an employee should remain competence and a willingness to work hard—not an organizationally correct ideology.

E x e r c i s e

Suppose you work in a liberal, pro-Clinton, pro-choice company. The ideal job candidate appears for an interview. Unfortunately, he or she is conservative, pro-Limbaugh, and pro-life. What is your action?

a. Hire the candidate anyway and brainwash him or her.

b. Reject the candidate because of your philosophical differences.

c. Hire the candidate and get on with business.

d. Buy Rush Limbaugh's latest book to see if you're the one with mistaken beliefs.

■ Business is a tough game played by grown-ups. There will be times when you need to play hardball—for example, you may have to shut down a factory and move manufacturing to a foreign country to lower costs. Can you and the employees who have been attracted to your socially responsible company make these kinds of decisions?

Despite these potential pitfalls, when you have a genuine interest in a social cause or philanthropic endeavor that ties in well with your company, pursue the possibility of doing something good for society to drive your competition crazy.

If there isn't an obvious way to link your company and your efforts to do good, then don't seek publicity. Just be a Good Samaritan, and in time the rewards will come. Even if they don't, you've still made the world a better place to live. And *you* live here.

Interview: Steve Scheier

S ay what you will about Steve Jobs, the cofounder of Apple Computer, he does come up with interesting ideas. In 1982 he decided that kids should learn how to use personal computers in elementary school. The person at Apple who implemented this idea was Steve Scheier. The program was called Kids Can't Wait.

This interview with Scheier shows you what really goes on when a company tries to do something good for society and help its business interests. As you'll see, such efforts are usually not a clear-cut case of crass commercialism or idealistic philanthropy. They're both.

Q: What motivated Apple to implement Kids Can't Wait?

The program was motivated by two things: the first was Steve's desire to get technology in the schools. He has always said that when he was growing up, there weren't computers.

The second motivation was to propel the growth of the market. Many years later I would go around to various schools in California, and invariably all those people remembered the program. Apple was indelibly seared in their minds because of this program, and in some cases educators could even show me the computers that they still had. The program really heartened people.

Q: Weren't there tax credits that reduced the true cost of the program? Would Steve Jobs have done it even if there weren't tax credits?

Our program costs were about $5 million, but after the tax credit, it only cost us $1 million. So, although there were costs inherent in the program, much of the cost was borne by the state in the form of a tax credit.

Knowing Steve, the answer is probably yes, he would have still done it. I think that having a tax credit just made it more financially palatable.

Q: Was Steve so forward-thinking that he felt teachers and students would fall in love with Apple's products and become a word-of-mouth marketing force?

Yes, absolutely, but I don't think we completely knew what was going to happen. We had our suspicions, certainly, but we really didn't know what was going to happen.

Q: How did the rest of the company feel?

The great majority of the company was really excited about it and really happy. People at Apple wanted to make a difference and saw this as a terrific opportunity to change the world and move forward.

The only group that was against it was the educational sales reps; their point of view was that it would ruin their markets.* Of course, two years later both of those guys retired as millionaires because, in fact, the market expanded tremendously.

Q: Rumor has it that you and Steve disagreed on implementation. What happened?

I wanted to give the computers to the districts and let the districts disperse them, but Steven went absolutely nuts when he heard this. He said I was completely crazy, and that he would never allow that. It had to be one computer per school. I said, "Steve, they'll never agree to that," but he was right. They did agree to it.

You want to stay close to the end user or customer. Steve felt if we gave them to the districts, God knows what might happen to them, but if we pushed them into the schools, there was a better chance that they would wind up serving kids.

---

*Another fine example of instinct overpowering intellect.

Q: Other companies also donated computers to schools. Why didn't they succeed?

The IBM, Tandy, and H-P programs all came out before ours. We were really concerned they were going to steal our thunder. As it turned out, it's not that they were badly executed. It was just that they didn't capture the imagination of the school people.

IBM's program, and pretty much all the other computer companies' programs, were "model-school programs." IBM's point of view was, "We'll show you how to set this thing up, and we're going to make donations to a select number of schools where we're going to pour in an enormous amount of hardware. They'll be model schools."

Apple's approach was more egalitarian. There was something exciting about every school getting a computer. The lesson is: if you're going to drive your competition crazy, seize the big idea. IBM had a lot of marketing muscle and sales muscle, but it didn't have a big idea. What it had were model schools.

Model schools was not a big idea. Give a computer to every school—that was a big idea. Seize the high ground and come up with a new and dynamite program.

Notes

[1]Judith Dobrzynski, "Impressionism Rides a Rental Car," *Business Week*, 9 May 1994, 52.

[2]*Business Ethics*, May-June 1992, 38.

[3]Paula Lyons, "Doing Good by Doing Well," *Ladies Home Journal*, September 1994, 112.

[4]*Business Ethics*, July-August 1990, 9.

[5]Joseph Pereira, " 'Liked the Lesson, and Loved the Shoes,' " *Wall Street Journal*, 25 August 1994, B1.

[6]Don Phillipson, "Everybody Wins," *Business 94*, December/January 1994, 46.

Part Three

Do Things

Right

To keep your competition hopelessly insane, it's not enough to do the right things. You must also do things right. Part III explains the four components of doing things right:

- Build customer allegiance early and often (Chapter 9, Establish Brand Loyalty).

- Magnify small chinks in your enemy's armor into gaping holes (Chapter 10, Make Mountains Out of Molehills).

- Eliminate your competition by befriending it,

rather than destroying it (Chapter 11, Make the Competition into a Friend).

- Repel the behemoths who try to muscle in on your territory (Chapter 12, Carry a Slingshot).

Establish Brand Loyalty

Treating a competitor's brand as if it didn't exist doesn't mean your customers will do the same.

Margie Smith, senior vice president, Mark Ponton Corporation

Reverse Polish Notation

When I graduated from high school in 1972, the state of the art of calculators was a slide rule. In college a few years later, I saw an electronic calculator for the first time. It was an H-P 35 calculator made by Hewlett-Packard that could add, subtract, multiply, and divide.

It used an unfamiliar logic called Reverse Polish Notation (RPN). If you wanted to add two numbers together, you would key in the first one, press the Enter key, key in the second one, and then press the +key, like this: 2 Enter 2 +.

Other calculators quickly entered the market, and most of them used algebraic notation. With an algebraic notation calculator, you would key in the first number, press the + key, key in the second number, and then press the =key, like this: 2 + 2 =.

Since the H-P 35, I've owned an H-P 65, H-P 41, H-P 92, and H-P 12c calculator, all of which used Reverse Polish Notation logic. I became accustomed to Reverse Polish Notation in college, so I've stuck with Hewlett-Packard's calculators since then.

The point of this tale is not to date myself. It is an illustration that one way to drive your competition crazy is to establish brand loyalty with customers while they are young or new to the marketplace.

E x e r c i s e

Analyze the goods and services you use. How many are what you started using when you were young and never changed since then? Are there goods and services that are better suited to your needs?

Systematize the Process

If I had first used an algebraic calculator, I would probably be loyal to no company in particular because the calculator market can be divided into two segments: Hewlett-Packard with RPN, and everybody else. In a sense, though, my loyalty to Hewlett-Packard calculators was a function of the H-P 35 being the first calculator on the market, not anything Hewlett-Packard did to establish brand loyalty.

It's much better to systematize building brand loyalty than to depend on luck or being first on the market. Good businesspeople make their own luck anyway. For example, Dick's Supermarkets, a chain of eight markets in Wisconsin and Illinois, uses a comprehensive direct-mail program to establish brand loyalty with new customers.

Store employees create a list of people who recently moved into the area, newly married couples, and families with newborn children. These lists are compiled from newspaper announcements, utility company new-account information, chambers of commerce announcements, and personal knowledge.

Newly arrived and newly married couples receive a welcome or congratulations letter from the general manager of the nearest Dick's store. There are six coupons included with the letter that are good for two free items each week for three weeks. "If we can bring people in six times we feel we can convert them into regular customers," says William Brodbeck, the president of Dick's Supermarkets.

Two and a half weeks after the first letter, Dick's sends a second letter from Brodbeck, another six coupons, and a self-addressed, postage-paid survey about the store. In this letter Brodbeck thanks people for using the coupons. How does he track coupon usage? He doesn't. He assumes that the recipients have used the coupons and sends this thank-you letter to all of them.

Finally, one year after the first letter is sent, Dick's sends a third letter with another survey and a coupon for a discount on items such as baked goods or flowers.

Newborn children receive a letter containing coupons that starts out with "This is your first business letter." Parents can redeem the coupons, and on the child's first birthday, a letter is sent to his or her parents along with a coupon for $2 off a birthday cake from Dick's.[1]

Start Early

Hewlett-Packard and Dick's Supermarkets illustrate the value of getting to customers early—whether early means as soon as they move into a geographic area or as soon as they're born. Forward-thinking companies create programs to attract and keep children as customers whenever feasible. These companies have figured out that children represent three markets in one:

- A primary market with spending money that can make its own choices

- A secondary market that influences the spending of their parents

- A future market that can patronize a company in the future as their income increases

Best Western International, Inc., has generating brand loyalty early down to a science. The hotel chain nabs customers at an early age through its Young Travelers Club, a promotion targeting kids ages eight to twelve.

When kids stay with their parents at a Best Western, they sign up for the club and receive a membership card, an "adventure journal" to record their travels, and an "adventure pack." The pack contains cards with historical information about states, a kids' travel magazine, decals, and other fun stuff.

For every dollar that club members or their parents spend at the hotel, they earn a point toward items from a catalog of goodies. Parents also accumulate points for their children. Some Best Western locations plan to open a young travelers' room, which might include anything from children's books and magazines to electronic games.[2]

"It's a lot less expensive to invest in kids now than to invest in adults once they've made up their minds," says Deborah Morehead, director of marketing, planning, and development for GS America, the company that developed the idea for the Young Travelers Club.

Tom Dougherty, Best Western International's manager of leisure and incentive markets, admits, "The motivator is to grow the next generation of Best Western customers." Dougherty also mentions that children have a great deal of influence on parental buying and decision-making.

The program builds Best Western's database of customers, and kids will be tracked through the years, in the hope of eventually transferring them to a Best Western frequent-business-traveler program.

Target Cubbyholes

One of the easiest ways to establish brand loyalty is to target cubbyholes of customers. Most companies use broad-brush marketing that is designed to appeal to everyone but usually ends up appealing to no one. This leaves cubbyholes wide open for you.

For example, Polaroid established brand loyalty in the real-estate broker cubbyhole with a program called the Polaroid Real Estate Photography Workshop. Realtors who attend the workshop receive instruction on how to use photography to better serve their customers.

Attendees are taught that photographs are an excellent way to keep a house fresh in the minds of customers and to help them visualize what living in the house would be like. Of course, if the attendees buy into this, they will have to use film—preferably Polaroid's—in the future.

Attendees pay $10 and receive a 600 Business Edition Camera, film, and an instruction booklet. Attendees also get a membership in Polaroid Preferred, a program for Polaroid special offerings and discounts.

Polaroid creates brand loyalty in three ways. First, its product delivers results. Real-estate brokers need pictures that they can immediately hand to prospects. Second, brokers are appreciative of the special attention they receive from Polaroid. They feel wanted. Third, brokers gain familiarity with Polaroid products. While other companies make similar film and cameras, most brokers don't know this, and they're not going to spend time figuring it out.

You may be wondering how a cubbyhole differs from a niche. A niche is usually determined on the basis of a product's characteristics— for example, speed, cost, size, or ease of use. Generally, these characteristics are objective, measurable, and apparent. By contrast, a cubbyhole is not determined by a product's characteristics but by the customers in the specific market. Thus, cubbyholes are vertical markets like real-estate brokers, doctors, teachers, or housewives.

A shameful, though illustrative, example of a cubbyhole occurred in the automotive market in 1932. Cadillac could not sell its high-priced cars, so General Motors was close to abandoning the division.[3] Nick Dreystadt was in charge of service for the whole country, and he noticed that many Cadillacs were brought in for service by wealthy blacks. This was surprising because it was against company policy to sell the car to blacks.

Apparently these Cadillac owners—for example, black entertainers, sports figures, doctors, and realtors—considered a Cadillac a status symbol, so they paid white people to buy the cars for them. Unable to purchase upscale housing and barred from luxury resorts, these consumers considered a Cadillac one of the few obtainable—albeit with some difficulty— outward symbols of success.

Dreystadt convinced General Motors' management to keep the Cadillac division going and to let him develop the sales of Cadillacs to blacks.

By 1934, only two years later, the division was breaking even because Dreystadt had successfully tapped this cubbyhole.

Cocoon Your Customers

Once you've fostered brand loyalty, it's a shame to lose it. Some factors can be controlled—for example, by maintaining a commitment to service and product development. Some factors—such as customers moving out of a geographic area—can't.

Smart companies build cocoons around their existing customers—shielding them from their competition and making them feel warm and fuzzy. They use what's called "frequency marketing" techniques that increase the use of a product or service and ensure that customers keep coming back. Here are three examples of effective frequency marketing programs from a frequency-marketing newsletter called *Colloquy*:

- The *New York Times* created a program called the Transmedia TimesCard for home-delivery subscribers. The program is designed to reduce cancellation by prepaid, home-delivery customers by offering reasons to maintain a subscription. Members of the TimesCard program receive discounts from restaurants and other businesses in New York City. For example, Lutece, the famous restaurant, offers a free serving of its soufflé to cardholders.[4]

- Federal Express operates the ExpressPlan program. To join, customers pay a $25 annual fee. They receive 100 points for every $25 of qualified shipments. Customers can use the points to select from a catalog of Federal Express discounts, travel, dining, office equipment, and gifts. Federal Express has found that sweepstakes and contests resulted in short-term sales, but that its frequency-marketing program yielded better long-term results.[5]

- Arby's is one of the first fast-food retailers to implement a frequency-marketing program. Customers join Club Arby's by filling out an enrollment form. They present a membership card and accumulate points for Arby's foods as well as merchandise and services from companies like Universal Studios and Minit-Lube. One Arby's franchisee in Sacramento, California, believes Club Arby's has doubled his repeat business.[6]

Exercise

If you don't have a frequency-marketing program, choose the reason why:

a. I never thought of it.

b. I'm lazy.

c. I'm a bozo.

d. I don't value repeat business.

Guidelines for Success

With hundreds of frequency-marketing efforts being implemented around the world, guidelines for successful programs are beginning to emerge:

- Establish your goal.

Usually frequency-marketing programs are established to *increase* business from existing customers. If your customers were probably going to patronize your business anyway, then you may be wasting money on discounts and gifts. If, however, your goal is to create good feelings about your company, then a frequency-marketing program that doesn't increase business is appropriate.

- Provide a complete product line.

Don't expect to create and maintain brand loyalty if you're not filling most of the customer's needs. For example, no matter how much people like an airline's mileage program, it won't foster brand loyalty unless the

119

airline serves the cities they need to visit. It's hard to be loyal to an incomplete product line.

- Maintain high-quality standards.

In an interview in *Colloquy*, Mike Gunn, senior vice president of marketing at American Airlines, stated, " . . . we never made the mistake of assuming that free trips could overcome bad service."[7] Frequency-marketing programs enhance good relationships, but they are not a substitute for good products and services. No matter how good Federal Express's frequency-marketing program, you wouldn't use the company unless your packages were delivered on time.

- Create multiple status levels.

I am a member of many airlines' frequent-flyer programs, but I always try to fly on United Airlines because I want to achieve Premier Executive status (a minimum of fifty thousand miles of travel per year). The primary benefit of this status is that I can upgrade to first class with inexpensive coupons seventy-two hours before my flight. Lower status levels can upgrade twenty-fours before a flight, but by then the first-class seats are usually all taken. The existence of the Premier level encourages me to patronize United on a consistent basis.

- Balance hard and soft benefits.

A hard benefit is quantifiable: discounts, free travel, and merchandise. A soft benefit is less tangible: special phone numbers, restricted check-in lines, and free gift wrapping—things that make customers feel like people, not numbers. Hard benefits may not adquately communicate how important a customer is to a company, and competitors can usually match or one-up hard benefits, causing a destructive me-too war. The answer: Provide both hard and soft benefits to create the right gestalt in your customer's mind.

- Keep it simple.

Frequency-marketing programs have a simple goal: fostering a long-term relationship. They should communicate a simple message: the more business a customer gives a company, the more the company appreciates it. Creating a complex program ("If you fly on Mondays or Fridays during leap years and stay a Saturday night . . . ") obfuscates* the bond between a company and its customers.

- Provide unique benefits.

Many products fill people's needs, and as more companies introduce frequency-marketing programs, it is more difficult to attract and retain customers—unless you provide something unique. Road Runner Sports, a sporting goods company, encourages members of its club to send in their old running shoes and a survey of their running habits, which the company then examines and utilizes to recommend specific shoes.[8]

Exercise

What are the effects of the following actions upon a company's current customers?

a. Phone companies that offer better deals to new customers than existing customers

b. Magazines that offer better deals to new subscribers than existing subscribers

c. Software companies that charge more for an upgrade than you originally paid for the software

Un-cocooning Your Competition's Customers

Aggressive business people not only cocoon their own customers, they also un-cocoon their competition's. The key to liberating your competition's customers is patience: don't try to create an immediate and

*Isn't "obfuscates" a nice touch in a paragraph called "Keep it simple"?

permanent shift. The first step is to catalyze a change in consumer habits via a trial of your product.

Introducing a successful trial means removing the costs of even a temporary change. Let's take a worst-case example: flying on a competitive airline, which means a customer would have to forego mileage that would have accrued on his or her current airline's program.

Virgin Atlantic figured out a way to solve this problem. It encouraged British Airways' customers to send in their BA Executive Club USA mileage program statement. If they had over ten thousand miles, they would qualify for free companion tickets for business-class and first-class seats. If they had less than ten thousand miles, Virgin matched the mileage, one for one, in its frequent-flyer program.

Once customers had tried Virgin Atlantic, they were much more likely to continue using the airline. The first trial, then, was a crucial step in wooing customers away from British Airways. Virgin's plan to un-cocoon the customers of British Airways surely drove British Airways nuts.

No matter how you do it, find ways to establish brand loyalty as early and as quickly as you can. Get so close to your customer that your competition doesn't have an opening—and watch your competition fly off the deep end.

Notes

[1]Murray Raphel, *Mind Your Own Business!* (Atlantic City, N.J.: Raphel Publishing, 1989), 104–107.

[2]Kerissa Hollis, "Best Western Aims to Rope Young Travelers," *Memphis Business Journal*, 3 January 1994, 23.

[3]Peter Drucker, *Adventures of a Bystander* (New York: Harper & Row, 1978), 268–69.

[4]"Frequency Marketing: A Sign of the Times," *Colloquy* 3, No. 3 (1993): 10–11.

[5]"Expressplan Absolutely, Positively Reaches Best Customers," *Colloquy* 4, No. 2 (1993): 1, 5.

[6]"Club Arby's: 'Different is Good,'" *Colloquy* 4, No. 2 (1993): 12–13.

[7]"A Candid conversation with Frequent-Flyer Pioneer Mike Gunn of American Airlines," *Colloquy* 3, No. 2 (1992): 9.

[8]"Road Runner Sports Chooses Relationships," *Colloquy* 4, No. 1 (1993): 1, 7.

Chapter 10

Make Mountains Out of Molehills

Great companies make meaning.

Richard Pascale, *The Art of Japanese Management*

The Smaller Footprint Wins

For decades, retailers have done their best to bash one another while wooing the American consumer. In particular, Sears, Roebuck and Company and Montgomery Ward competed fiercely with each other because they both used mail-order catalogs to reach people living in rural areas.

Aaron Montgomery Ward started the company that bears his name in 1872. Richard Sears started Sears, Roebuck and Company approximately twenty years later. However, after only eight years Sears surpassed Montgomery Ward as the largest mail-order company in the United States,[1] and for the next forty years, Sears dominated the competition between the two retailing giants.[2]

Their warlike struggle yields an important lesson about making mountains out of molehills. Imagine you're a farmer sitting in your kitchen. You like mail-order catalogs because they enable you to avoid the monopoly of local merchants.

You reach over for a catalog because you need shoes, furniture, fishing tackle, or clothes. There are two catalogs in a pile: one from Sears and one from Montgomery Ward.

Which one do you grab first? The one on top. Which one is on top? The one with the smaller footprint. Why is the smaller one on top? Because if you put the larger one on the smaller one, it is likely to slide off. Richard Sears figured out this simple, insightful bit of molehillism and made his catalog smaller than Montgomery Ward's.

This chapter explains how to find or create little features of your product or service—molehills—and make them into mountains that differentiate you from your competition.

By the way, Richard Sears was an entrepreneur's entrepreneur. One of his first merchandising efforts occurred while he was a railroad station agent in North Redwood, Minnesota, in 1886. A jewelry company incorrectly shipped a case of gold-filled watches to a jeweler, and the jeweler refused the shipment.[3] Richard Sears looked at the watches before sending them back and decided he could sell them. He seized the day, telegraphed other station agents along the railroad line, and sold all the watches for a nice profit. Arguably, this was the first successful telemarketing campaign.[4]

Richard Sears may also have been the first multilevel marketer. To increase the size of the Sears catalog mailing list, he asked his best customers to distribute catalogs to twenty-four friends and relatives. To reward their efforts, he gave them points that could be used to get free merchandise when the recipients placed an order—making evangelists out of customers.

Assume Nothing

A fascinating and sometimes frustrating quality of molehills is that they seem small or insignificant until you or your competitor has made them into mountains, and then they seem obvious and after-the-fact—like the solution to this puzzle.

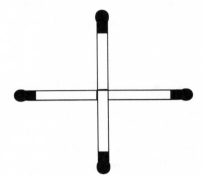

Move one match to make a square.[5]

Give up? One answer is to pull down the match at the six o'clock position to create a square hole at the center of the figure. Another answer is to use the match at the three o'clock position and connect the end points of the matches at the twelve o'clock and nine o'clock positions to make a "4." Four is the square of two.*

Why don't most people think of these solutions? Because they assumed they had to creat a square whose *sides* were formed by the matches or that "square" was meant in the shape, not multiplication, sense. Therein lies the secret to finding good molehills to drive your competition crazy: Assume nothing and look under your nose.

Be Your Customer

I admit that an admonishment like "Assume nothing and look under your nose" is not specific enough to generate action. Let me get very specific: To appreciate your advantage put yourself in your customer's shoes. Two stories about children illustrate the value of this principle.

First, a young girl bought gumdrops from a small shop even though a more convenient supermarket opened nearby. Asked why, the girl said, "Nick [the store owner] always gives me more candy. The girl in the other

---

*This solution was contributed by Steve Kopp when he read this book. I would have never thought of it. Kudos!

store takes some away." Apparently salesclerks in the supermarket put more than the weight, and then the clerks subtracted a few gumdrops to get the right amount. Nick, the owner of the small shop, put in too little and then added more. The children were convinced they got a better deal from Nick.[6]

Exercise

You have a choice of two gas stations. One charges $1.50/ gallon of gas but gives a $.10/gallon discount for cash. The other charges $1.40/gallon but tacks on an additional $.10/gallon for credit card purchases. Which station would you rather buy gas from?*

Second, a school in Virginia had trouble filling a course called "Home Economics for Boys." Considering the title, this isn't too surprising. Putting themselves in the place of the students, the school renamed the class "Bachelor Living," and 120 boys immediately signed up.

These stories illustrate how putting yourself in your customer's shoes helps you understand how to appeal to them. Imagine for a moment that you are Richard Sears: What kinds of molehills would you use to make customers prefer your catalog? How about stocking XXL size clothes, using larger print for easier to read copy, or providing tidbits from the *Old Farmer's Almanac*?

The point is that when you assume the role of your customers and intuit their needs, then finding molehills becomes easy. As further guidance, molehills usually fall into three simple categories: eliminating headaches, saving money, and making packaging into a weapon.

Eliminate Headaches

When customers of Servtech, a car-repair shop located in a suburb of Minneapolis, want to change the oil in their cars, they don't have to

---

*Inspired by *The Strategy and Tactics of Pricing* by Thomas Nagle and Reed Holden. Most people respond that they would rather buy gas from the service station that discounts for cash rather than charges a premium for credit card use.

arrange for a ride to and from the shop or wait to get service.* All they have to do is get a good night's sleep.

This is because Servtech sends an employee to pick up the customers' cars at their homes and drive them to the shop for oil and lubrication changes. Servtech then returns the cars to its customers by 6:00 the next morning.[7]

Similarly, when customers at Alaska's Northrim bank want to make a deposit, they don't have to take the time to drive to the bank. Business customers making noncash deposits or delivering documents to the bank can use a courier service for a mere dollar per pickup.

Northrim president Marc Langland told the *Alaska Journal of Commerce* that the service is part of the bank's ongoing strategy of providing convenient customer services that set it apart in the marketplace—particularly for small business customers who cannot afford to be away from their companies.[8]

We're not talking rocket science here: Servtech and Northrim illustrate that simple actions taken to eliminate your customer's headaches can differentiate you from your competition and foster loyalty. The message is clear: *Think of problems that aggravate potential customers and solve them.*

Save Money

Another common type of molehill is to provide ways for your customers to save money. Toll-free phone lines, postage-paid envelopes, and free shipping are the most common examples of this kind of molehill.

Ameritech, the $20 billion telephone company in the Midwest, provides a more creative example. It invented a new kind of call-waiting signal. Customers who subscribe to this service hear two kinds of beeps: the usual one that signals an incoming call and a new one that signals an incoming long-distance call.†[9]

This enables Ameritech customers to distinguish the type of call that is coming in and have the option for answering long-distance calls rather

---

*How many times have you ever made it out of a nine-minute lube shop in nine minutes?

†Now if Ameritech could only invent another beep for unwanted calls, I'd move to the Midwest.

than returning these calls at their expense. Thus, Ameritech customers can save money on long-distance charges and reduce telephone tag with callers in other time zones. If you had the choice between a telephone carrier with this feature and others that didn't, which carrier would you use?

Make Packaging into a Weapon

The final category of molehill is using packaging as a weapon—not merely a graphic design or a component of costs of goods sold. Here are four examples:

- ComponentGuard, Inc. of Valhalla, New York, sells extended warranties for consumer electronics. Its product isn't a tangible object, like a VCR or stereo, but this doesn't mean that the product has to be invisible. The company put its service contract and membership card in a plastic package that hangs from retail racks.[10]

- Chubs Stackable baby wipes, manufactured by L&F Products of Montvale, New Jersey, come in a colorful plastic container. These Lego-like boxes are interlockable and come in four bright colors. Babies play with the boxes as if they were big plastic toys. Parents can use the containers for knickknacks or refill them with more baby wipes.[11]

- Amurol Confections Company of Naperville, Illinois, sells a plastic jar filled with candy tarts called Bug City. The lid of the jar is perforated, so that kids can use the jar to keep bugs in.[12]

- Reed Plastic Containers in England markets a clear plastic paint container to paint companies. The container is square with rounded corners to facilitate stacking, and the paint color is easy to see because the container is clear. There is a brush wiping area, a built-in lip for pouring, and the handle is off-center to enable customers to easily dip a paintbrush.[13]

ComponentGuard went from selling an intangible guarantee to selling a product you could touch and feel. Chubs and Amurol Confections took the principle one step further: their packaging enhances their customers' lives in a small way by extending the use of its products. Reed Plastic Containers made painting easier from the time you buy the product until the time you store it away.

When you make packaging a weapon, all you're trying to do is gain an unfair advantage, no matter how small, at the moment when a customer is making up his or her mind: "If I buy Chubs, Bam Bam can play with the box. If I buy another brand, he can't."

Make Mountains Out of Mountains

Once you've made a mountain out of a molehill, the last step is to make a mountain out of a mountain—that is, ensure that the world knows what you've done. Marketing experts at Regis McKenna, Inc., a public relations firm in Silicon Valley, have perfected a technique to do this.

They call it "outrageous substitute positioning."* To understand it, you first need to understand the two types of traditional positioning: first, positioning your product as creating a category; second, positioning your product as different in an existing category.

The original Sony Walkman, for example, created a category of personal electronic devices. Other category-creating products include Polaroid's instant camera (1947), Bulova's electronic watch (1960), and Raytheon's microwave oven (1947).

The Jeep Grand Cherokee is an example of a product that wasn't the first in its category—sports utility vehicles—but is one that is very different from its competition. The fact that the Grand Cherokee was the first sports utility vehicle with an airbag and carlike handling established it as the leader in its category.

Glenn Helton, a partner at Regis McKenna, describes the making-a-mountain-out-of-a-mountain technique:

> The outrageous substitute approach involves comparing a new product from one category to an established product from a distinctly

*I learned about outrageous substitute positioning by reading a document that Regis McKenna, Inc., had posted on eWorld, an electronic bulletin board. This proves there are some things of value on the information highway.

Exercise

Can't come up with any molehills? Answering these questions may help.

- **What would cause your customer to use more of your product at each occasion?**

- **What would cause your customer to use your product on more occasions?**

- **What would cause your distribution channels to stock more of your product?**

- **What is the most fun your customers ever had with your product?**

- **How can you institutionalize having fun with your product?**

Still can't come up with any? I'll give you some that would make me patronize a company.

- **A razor whose blade won't come off when I throw it in a shaving kit and carry it around the country**

- **An airline whose airplanes have power outlets at the seats for using a portable computer**

- **A restaurant that provides beepers to customers so that they can put their names on the waiting list and go off and shop and do errands until their tables are ready**

---

different category. In effect, a company positions its product as an "outrageous substitute" for a respected product in a different, and usually higher-end, category.

Toyota's introduction of the Lexus line of cars is an example of outrageous substitute positioning. These cars were squarely positioned against Mercedes and BMW. The outrageous statement Toyota made was that its new marque with no track record in luxury cars was as good as or better than the industry standards at far less cost.

Did Toyota's outrageous substitute positioning hurt the sales of Mercedes or BMW? Probably not in the first several years, but without a doubt Toyota established Lexus as a luxury car marque, and it did make sales to thousands of people who couldn't or wouldn't pay for a Mercedes or BMW.

According to Helton, in order for outrageous substitute positioning to work, this condition must be present:

> There has to be enough credibility—not to prove the main substitution claim—but to establish a dialogue about the product within the marketplace.... In effect, the marketplace's response to the outrageous substitution claim does not have to be "Yes, I agree," as much as "Tell me more about what you mean."

As you create your mountains, think of how you can position them as outrageous substitutes to get the most mileage out of what you've done. Northrim could position its $1 messenger service against owning a car; Ameritech could position its call-waiting feature against a telephone receptionist; and the manufacturer of Chubs could position its baby-wipes packaging against expensive Lego blocks.

Exercise

Match the product or service in the first column to an outrageous positioning in the second column.

Taxi service	**Going to the game**
San Diego	**Personal visit**
Greeting card	**Owning a car**
Cable TV sports channel	**Poipu Beach**

Interview: Jay Levinson

In a nutshell, guerrilla marketing is the process of finding and exploiting molehills, and Jay Levinson is to guerrilla marketing what Tom Peters is to excellence, Al Ries and Jack Trout to positioning, and John Grisham to legal thrillers.

Levinson made guerrilla marketing a genre in business books because he wrote *Guerrilla Marketing, Guerrilla Marketing Attack, Guerrilla Marketing Excellence, Guerrilla Advertising*, and co-wrote *The Guerrilla Marketing Handbook, Guerrilla Financing*, and *Guerrilla Selling*. Get the idea? He is The Man when it comes to making molehills into mountains.

Q: Are guerrilla marketers born or made?

Guerrilla marketers are made. It's too hard to be born with the comprehensiveness that a true guerrilla needs. It's asking too much of a person to be that broad in scope.

Everybody can become a guerrilla marketer, but not everybody can do all the functions necessary. Some may have to delegate a lot of the functions; some may have to delegate just a few. The idea is knowing what has to be done and then causing it to be done. Whether you or someone else does it doesn't matter.

Q: What are the traits a guerrilla marketer must have?

The first one is patience. If you expect things to happen too fast, there's going to be too much frustration along the way. The truth is lots of great marketing has been created and then abandoned.

The second is imagination in terms of the options of marketing. It's not a matter of what kind of headline or what kind of feature. It's understanding weapons of marketing—which ones you use, how you use them, and timing.

The third is sensitivity to everything—to the market, to your competition, to your customers, to your employees, to the time in history, and the state of the economy. You can't have a preconceived, cast-in-bronze attitude and be insensitive to what else is happening and how well your attitude fits in with reality.

The fourth is a love of learning. You've got to keep learning because things keep changing. If you're not keeping up, then you're falling behind. You can't judge the future by the past anymore, and with some things, you get to make it up as you go along.

The fifth is ego strength, because if you do everything right, the first people who will get tired of what you're doing are your partners, spouse, and best friends. However, your prospects aren't bored, and your customers will never be bored—they'll always read what you put out to justify that they do business with you. The only people who will be bored are the people who matter the most in your life and the least in your business.

The last is aggressiveness—in two areas. Area one is spending. How much does the average U.S. business invest in marketing? Last year they say the number was 4 percent. A guerrilla's attitude is, "Is that all? What if I put in 8 percent?"

The other aggressiveness is the realization that when you learn there are a hundred different weapons or more, you think, Wow, look how many things I get to do—and so many of these are free!

Q: What are the decisive functions for a guerrilla marketer?

Number one, by far, is follow-up. Writing a thank-you note within forty-eight hours can be practiced by large and small companies. Follow a month later with a letter to make sure they're happy with the purchase they made and to see if they have any questions.

Three months later, send a letter mentioning other things that they may want to purchase that are related to what they bought in the first place. Nine months later send a questionnaire and apologize that you're asking so many questions, but the more you know about them, the better service you can provide.

Then you get back to them again and ask them for the name of three people who might benefit from getting on your mailing list. You might go as far as sending an anniversary card on the one-year anniversary of their purchase, but you always stay in touch with them.

If you do follow-up, you'll drive your competition crazy because they're not doing it. Hardly anybody does it. Sixty-eight percent of business lost in America is lost because of the apathy after the sale. Not poor service. Not poor quality, but the love-'em-and-leave-'em attitude. This means there's lots of room to move on in.

Number two is fusion marketing. This occurs when you get involved with other companies and strategic alliances: "I'll enclose your brochure in my next mailing if you enclose my brochure in your next mailing." "Let's get a regional ad in *Time* and share the cost."

Fusion marketing lets you increase the marketing exposure and decrease the marketing costs. You're gaining partners. Your competition sees your name in more places than he's ever seen it before. It's not costing you much, and he's asking, "Why didn't I think of that?"

Number three is spying—spying on yourself and your competitors, buying things from them, making requests of them, and doing the same for yourself—and seeing the differences. You try to prevent anybody from getting better than you. If they do get better than you, it won't be for long because you're going to find out about it and you're going to get better than they are.

Q: Any other guerrilla marketing techniques to drive your competition crazy?

I'd find out who your competitor's customers are and make those customers one of your target audiences. I would make a continual effort to talk to their customers and become part of their customers' lives. That would win a lot of their customers over because you're probably paying better attention to their customers than they are.

Q: What's the best guerrilla idea you ever heard?

Using ten stamps when you do a direct mailing instead of one stamp. Ten stamps still cost twenty-nine cents, if you get the right denominations of twos, three, and sixes, and it will assure that your letter will get opened because no one receives an envelope with ten stamps!

Guerrilla marketing requires time, energy, and imagination—not necessarily money. This is a good example. It takes time, energy, and imagination to put ten stamps on an envelope.

Notes

[1]Sandra S. Vance and Roy V. Scott, *Wal-Mart: A History of Sam Walton's Retail Phenomenon* (New York: Twayne Publishers, 1994), 20.

[2]Richard Tedlow, *New and Improved: The Story of Mass Marketing in America* (New York: Basic Books, 1990), 301.

[3]Jack Mingo, *How the Cadillac Got Its Fins* (New York: HarperCollins, 1994), 28.

[4]Ibid., 32.

[5]Martin Gardner, *More Perplexing Puzzles and Tantalizing Teasers* (New York: Dover Publications, Inc., 1969), 24.

[6]Peter Hay, *The Book of Business Anecdotes* (Avenel, N.J.: Wings Books, 1988), 104–105.

[7]Thomas Winninger, *Price Wars: How to Win the Battle for Your Customer* (Edina, Minn.: St. Thomas Press, 1994), 236.

[8]Rose Ragsdale, "Banks Hone Offerings to Meet Stiffer Competition," *Alaska Journal of Commerce*, 21 March 1994, 14.

[9]Gary Samuels, "A Meeting at the Breakers," *Forbes*, 20 June 1994, 56.

[10]Sarah Noble, ed., *301 Great Management Ideas from America's Most Innovative Small Companies* (Boston: Inc. Publishing, 1991), 119.

[11]Jay Levinson and Seth Godin, *The Guerrilla Marketing Handbook* (Boston: Houghton Mifflin Company, 1994), 253.

[12]Business Bulletin," *Wall Street Journal*, 8 September 1994, 1.

[13]"Best Products," *Management Today* (United Kingdom), December 1990, 65. As cited in Allan Magrath, *The 6 Imperatives of Marketing* (New York: American Management Association, 1992), 169.

Chapter 11

Make
the Competition
into a Friend

Soon after the Civil War, President Abraham Lincoln met with several Southerners. Expecting to despise the leader of the North, they ended up charmed by Lincoln's gentle and friendly manner. A congressman from a northern state reproached Lincoln for befriending them. Lincoln's response was: "Am I not destroying my enemies by making them my friends?"[1]

The Knight and the Dragon

During a trip to Hawaii my wife forced me to stop working on this book and visit the Honolulu Academy of Arts. A book called *The Knight and the Dragon* caught my eye at the Academy's exhibit of children's book illustrators.

This book, by a famous children's author named Tomie dePaola, explains how to renounce conventional expectations (a knight and a dragon must fight each other). DePaola's book shows how to make enemies into allies ("strategic alliances," in current business parlance) better than anything I've ever seen. Fortunately, he was kind enough to permit me to reprint his book in its entirety.

NOTE: The inclusion of *The Knight and the Dragon* illustrates the message of this chapter. DePaola and I have formed an alliance. He gets his book exposed to thousands of nose-to-the-grindstone business readers—some of whom will go out and buy his book in its full, glorious color version because this reprint won't do his handiwork justice.

I derive three benefits: First, I get to use a terrific story by a top-notch children's author; second, his work adds an unusual graphic element to a "business book"; and third, I don't have to write a chapter.

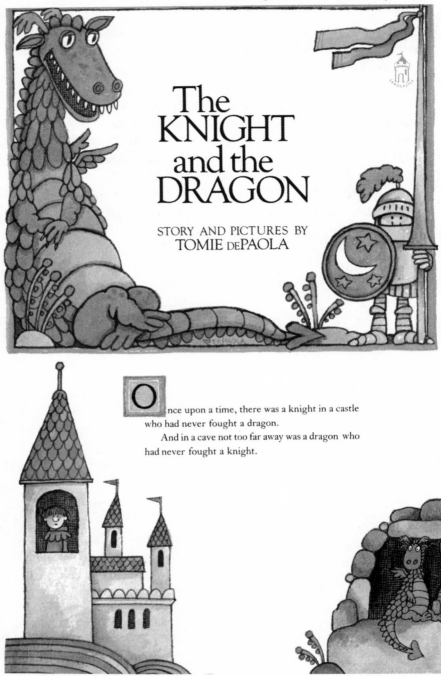

The KNIGHT and the DRAGON

STORY AND PICTURES BY
TOMIE dePAOLA

O nce upon a time, there was a knight in a castle who had never fought a dragon.

And in a cave not too far away was a dragon who had never fought a knight.

The Knight and the Dragon by Tomie dePaola, copyright © 1980 by Tomie dePaola. Reprinted by permission of G. P. Putnam's Sons.

One day the knight went to the castle library and took out all of the books he could find on dragon fighting.

Meanwhile, back at the cave, the dragon had rummaged through all the things from his ancestors and found some books on knight fighting.

145

147

151

"Coopetition" in Action

J ust so you don't think the story of *The Knight and the Dragon* is merely a fairy tale, I offer this genuine business example. In 1989, the Atcheson, Topeka and Santa Fe Railway shocked the trucking and railroad industries when it formed an alliance with a trucking company called J.B. Hunt Transport.[2]

Here's how the coopetition works between two former competitors. Hunt sends a truck to a shipping customer to pick up freight, puts the loaded truck trailer on a Santa Fe train, and the train hauls the trailer to the rail yard nearest the destination. Hunt retrieves its trailer and delivers the shipment. All of this process is accomplished with one bill.

Customers gain fast, door-to-door delivery at a reasonable price—something railroads have failed to provide. Hunt saves fuel plus driver and truck wear-and-tear. The railway gains business from a former competitor. In addition, the alliance reduces traffic, wear and tear on highways, and pollution.

This relationship marks a change in the traditionally hostile relationship between railroads and truck companies. In the past, they stole business from each other. Now they are forming alliances. As Will and Ariel Durant wrote in *The Lessons of History*,

> Co-operation is real, and increases with social development, but mostly because it is a tool and form of competition; we co-operate in our group—our family, community, club, church, party, 'race,' or nation—in order to strengthen our group in its competition with other groups.[3]

Be Thy Competition

O ne way to make the competition into a friend is to be the competition. Sly companies accomplish this by creating new brands that appear to be their own competition. Suzanne Oliver of *Forbes* explained how Black & Decker pulled this off with its DeWalt line of power tools.

According to Oliver, at the 1992 National Homebuilders Show, an attendee told Nolan Archibald, the chairman of Black & Decker, that "these guys are going to eat you up," as he was looking at a line of DeWalt power tools.

Archibald could only smile in response since DeWalt is manufactured by Black & Decker. The purpose of the DeWalt line is to attract professional and industrial users who eschew Black & Decker because the Black & Decker name is associated with do-it-yourselfers.

Joseph Galli, the Black & Decker employee who thought of the idea, upgraded some of the tools in the Black & Decker line and made them the bright yellow color that matches hard hats. He created a fleet of salespeople who called on construction sites and hardware stores in matching yellow-colored vans.

Finally, he raised the price of the DeWalt products above Makita's, the industry leader, to position his products above the competition's, and he controlled distribution so that DeWalt products would not appear in mass-market outlets. After two years on the market the DeWalt brand is expected to account for $300 million in sales.[4]

The practice of being your own competition—self-cannibalizing, if you will—belongs in the arsenal of anyone trying to drive his or her competition crazy. It doesn't always work, because employees may have difficulty adopting a different mind-set for pricing and quality, but it is guaranteed to send your competition off the deep end.

Note that self-cannibalization is a privilege. It implies that you have the luxury of capital, production, and personnel to achieve incremental sales. Thus, you earn the privilege by doing things right for your customers in the first place. As with many privileges, do not squander it—in this case by letting your competition cannibalize you before you cannibalize yourself.

Exercise

Write a one-page plan of how your competition could cannibalize you. Why couldn't you execute this plan against yourself?

Guidelines

Before you rush off to form alliances or partnerships of coopetition, be aware that they aren't a panacea for improving your business. If you don't have your act together, getting in bed with another organization is going to aggravate, not solve, your problems. These are the guidelines for turning enemies into friends:

- Keep your customer in mind. A relationship between former competitors might be good for both parties, but if it doesn't benefit your customer, it probably won't last long. This is to say that people had better like the flavor of K & D Bar-B-Q food.

- Ensure that both sides benefit. A one-sided relationship will not last very long. Even a relationship where one partner receives slightly more benefit is doomed. Two plus two must equal at least five for coopetition to work.

- Think of the relationship as dating, not marriage.* "Long-term alliance" is an oxymoron. When mutual benefits disappear, so will the relationship, so don't put too many eggs in this basket. Whether you consider the relationship as dating or marriage, sign a prenuptial agreement that documents how the relationship should end.

- Hating a common enemy is not reason enough to form a relationship. For example, Apple and IBM's partnership is founded more on a shared fear of Microsoft than on a concern for customers. Would you marry someone because you both disliked the same person?

- Build relationships from the bottom. Usually the worker bees find out about the relationship by reading the newspaper after two company presidents got together for a grand press conference. The worker bees, however, are the folks who make the relationship work.

- Beware of Trojan horses. A prospective partner may undertake or form an alliance in order to extract confidential information from you.

*Although with 50 percent of marriages ending in divorce, maybe you should consider it marriage.

154

This is industrial espionage, not a mutually beneficial relationship, so go slow and practice safe pacts.

Observing these guidelines, you can rid yourself of your competition by turning it into your ally. If a knight and a dragon can do this, so can you.

Notes

[1]Michael Green, ed., *Illustrations for Biblical Teaching* (Grand Rapids, Mich.: Baker Book House, 1989), 157.

[2]David Field, "Piggyback = Piggybank: Trains and Truckers Benefit When They Move the Goods Together," *The Washington Times*, 14 February 1993, A10–A11.

[3]Will and Ariel Durant, *The Lessons of History* (New York: Simon and Schuster, 1968), 19.

[4]Suzanne Oliver, "New Personality," *Forbes*, 15 August 1994, 114.

Chapter 12

Carry a Slingshot

My center is giving way, my right is pushed back; situation excellent, I am attacking.

Ferdinand Foch at the Second Battle of the Marne, 1918

Catch the Spirit

To prevent price shoppers from leaving his store and going to the competition, an appliance retailer gives potential customers half gallons of ice cream just for coming in. The retailer knows full well that if they go and shop at other stores, the ice cream will melt before they get home.[1]

When a pizza chain entered the Colorado market, it looked for ways to establish itself quickly and steal business from existing pizza parlors. It ran a promotion that offered two pizzas for the price of one if customers brought in its competitor's Yellow-Pages advertising.[2] Of course, the next time customers looked in the Yellow Pages, the competition's ad was gone.

What do these companies have in common? They both used a sling-shot—a deceptively simple, inexpensive, and effective weapon—against their competition. None of these companies, however, had a problem like Bob Curry.

In 1992 Curry learned that Home Depot—Goliath—was opening one of its superstores a mere quarter of a mile from his Ace Hardware store in Quincy, Massachusetts. For an independently owned hardware store, albeit of a national franchise, Home Depot is the mother of all competition. Until the arrival of this giant, Curry's store was a typical local hardware store in a quiet, small community.

Interview: Bob Curry

T he sign on the desk of Bob Curry says, "Raving Fans. Satisfied customers just aren't good enough." The back of the T-shirt that his store sells says, "Curry Hardware. The Store You Can't Forget." These two slogans sum up Curry's business: he has raving fans who can't forget his store.

Part of the reason why his customers can't forget is that Curry won't let them. After our interview, for example, he drove me to the Home Depot store. He spotted a customer of his pulling out of the parking lot and railed on him in a quasi-joking manner: "What are you doing shopping here?"

You may not own a hardware store, but the principles and techniques Bob utilized are relevant lessons for any business that's trying to drive its competition crazy. Now I'll let him tell you his story.

Lesson #1: Don't Panic

We were petrified of Home Depot because of the things we had read in the trade magazines and because we had talked to stores in Long Island, Atlanta, New Orleans, and Florida. Sales were dropping 20 to 25 percent in the first year!

We told ourselves we had to get our act together. We had to find a way to beat Home Depot and stop being afraid of it. Instead of going on the defense, we were going on the offense. We were just going to do what we knew how to do, do it right, and not worry about it.

We didn't want our people to be nervous wrecks. And we didn't want them to see that we were nervous wrecks! Everywhere we went, everybody was afraid for us. It was something that we heard several hundred times a day, seven days a week, for a year and a half before Home Depot opened.

We even had one person suggest that our store would be a nice chicken restaurant. Hardware stores all around our area—up to fifteen miles away—would call us and ask us what we were going to do because they figured we were going to be gone.

Lesson #2: Competition Is Good

Home Depot really got us off our rear ends. It got our blood boiling again and got our entrepreneurial juices flowing. We started scheming and figuring out what we had to do in pricing, advertising, and service.

We had to figure out a way to keep our key people and to find a niche. These were things we hadn't really done for a few years because we'd been busy while the economy was great all through the 1980s. Why weren't we doing it five or ten years ago? Because sometimes we all need a boot in the rear end, that's why. We needed something to wake us up, and Home Depot woke us up, I'll tell you.

How has Home Depot affected us? Other stores told us our sales would be off 25 percent the first year. The first few months sales were flat, and then they jumped up 4 or 5 percent. That first spring, which was only six months after the opening, our sales were up 12, 13, or 14 percent. Our sales for the first six months of this fiscal year have been up over 35 percent.

Lesson #3: Maintain Morale

We try to have a lot of fun here. We kid and fool around all day long. We pay well, and we've got a pension and profit-sharing package that most small businesses don't have. We try to have all those things to show our employees that it is worthwhile to work here.

Also, you can't have a staff with high morale if they're not trained. They have to be comfortable and know what they're doing, so we have a training room in the basement of the store where we show the videos we get from Ace.

Finally, we thank them. Thanking employees isn't always about money. There isn't a week that goes by that when I'm handing out the checks, I don't thank them for what they've done for us.

Lesson #4: Be Realistic

At hardware-store seminars where I spoke, we had guys come up and say, "Our customers are loyal." Baloney. Customers are loyal to nothing but their wallet. If you had to work real hard for sixty hours a week, are you going give a guy $49 when you can buy something for $29?

Customers won't be loyal for very long. They think the same way you and I do about our money. They're just as careful spending it, so you've got to create the right mind-set with people and show them that you can be competitive, and you can be fair.

Lesson #5: Do What's Right for the Customer

We try to get to know as many customers as we can in a personal way. Home Depot cannot do that. You can't have 150 employees in the store and 120,000 square feet of store and expect them to know their customers.

We never opened on Sundays because we had strange blue laws. Then, when stores started to open on Sundays, most of the small stores still didn't follow suit. Only the large stores did, but when Home Depot came in, we had to change.

It was a traumatic thing because we were used to having our Sundays off, but we're getting used to it now—or most of us are. I still haven't gotten used to it, but hours are very important. Hours are customer service.

The first couple of weeks we had seven people on because we didn't know what to expect. For maybe ten Sundays in a row, we did double what we'd done on any Saturday. During the summer things quieted down a little bit, but even now in July and August it's still very, very busy on a Sunday, so there was a need for it.

The most important thing is just servicing and servicing and servicing. A guy brought in an old wooden floor lamp. He wanted to put in a new socket and rewire the lamp, but the wooden part of it was all falling apart. We asked if he wanted us to fix it. He asked, "Can you do that?" You bet your life.

Lesson #6: Be Flexible

Pricing was a big thing. We wanted to make sure that people saw us as competitive. They didn't have to see us as being cheaper than Home Depot. It does $10 billion a year in sales, so people didn't expect us to be cheaper, but they expected to get a fair deal.

We took four hundred or five hundred items and gave them away. We picked all the most price-sensitive items—for example, Rustoleum, spray paint, and generic things like a gallon of paint thinner or light bulbs. We worked and worked on this for probably a year.

I wished we'd had two or three years to do it. We published lists of our everyday low prices, and we kept changing it. When Home Depot opened, we found we were cheaper on some of these prices, so we immediately marked all our prices up to match Home Depot's.

We didn't try to sell anything lower than Home Depot. We didn't tell anybody we had things cheaper than it—they wouldn't believe us anyway, so we just got our prices up to the same price, and we kept watching it.

One of the ways we showed people we had competitive prices was to use private labels. First, we priced General Electric bulbs at almost zero margin to match Home Depot's prices. However, all the Ace private-label light bulbs are made by General Electric, so we tell customers where they come from and then push the Ace brand. We make 25 to 30 percent margin on these bulbs yet they still retail for less money.

Lesson #7: Develop Niches

We came up with different niches. We read and researched every trade magazine we could get our hands on to see what other people were doing in different niches, why some of them worked, and why some of them didn't. Long before the customers really wanted something, we felt we had to come up with the right thing.

For example, we never sold propane before because we couldn't get a license, so we fought and fought for a license. Now we probably do $100,000 worth of sales in propane, and we've only been doing it about a year and a half.

We really opened up a paint department. We always had a lot of paint, but the paint was in the basement, on the first floor, and in the warehouse upstairs. We brought it all together and made it look like we were a paint store even though we probably didn't increase our volume of inventory that much.

We do a tremendous amount of servicing of Makita, Black & Decker, and DeWalt* power tools. We're authorized to do some warranty work on them. Now we even job out the repairs because we do so much of it.

Also, we probably tripled the amount of inventory we have in our fastener department. We still don't have as much as Home Depot, but it doesn't have anybody to wait on customers. Fasteners are a department that you need people to help you through—even the tradesmen need help.

On the other hand, we don't have everything that Home Depot has. We don't have a line of 200 faucets. We just don't have it, and we never will, so that's something we have to concede. We don't have a big lighting department either, so we're going to lose some of that business too.

Lesson #8: Know Thy Enemy

When Home Depot first opened, we were there at least once a week. They don't like you shopping their store for prices, so we carried voice-activated tape recorders† and we would take any kind of literature that we could find in the store.

---

*Which, as we found out in the previous chapter, are the same as Black & Decker power tools.
†Like Sam Walton's, only smaller.

Any time the managers saw us take stuff, they'd just smile. This stuff is not something top management wanted us to have, but the managers knew who we were so they'd just smile.

Lesson #9: Do Something for Your Community

I've been involved in the Rotary Club in Quincy for a long time and another small group—we call ourselves the Quincy Partnership. There's about fifteen of us. We try to do things to spruce the city up, and we've probably raised a hundred grand in the last couple of years to put up nice signage welcoming people to Quincy.

All this got me some good connections, and the connections were with people who I didn't really rub shoulders with that often, such as the president of the bank in the city. One small publication called *The Quincy Business News* is probably the best-read paper here in Quincy. We started getting big write-ups because John Graham, the publisher, is a customer.

He saw that a lot of the things we were doing were successful, and he liked those kinds of things because he was doing the same things in his own business, so he started writing about us. When Home Depot opened, the first issue had an article about Home Depot, and 75 percent of it was about Curry Hardware. It seems like every single issue has something about Curry Hardware.

Lesson #10: Make the Competition into a Friend

About a week ago, the new guy that's in charge of power tools at Home Depot came in and checked all our prices. He said our pricing was really good. The reason he came in, though, was that he was looking at how well we serve our customer. He told us that from now on they're going to send anyone with any kind of a service problem to us!

Customers who buy a gas grill at Home Depot ask employees there where they can get propane. Home Depot sends them right down to us. Hopefully, we capture them as customers. We make the customers go in the store to pay for the propane, which is stored outside, so they're forced to learn more about us.

We work hard to build some kind of a bond between Home Depot

162

and us rather than try to fight. Most of the people that we've talked to in other parts of the country wanted nothing to do with Home Depot. We felt we'd be better off if we worked with it. If Home Depot wanted to, it could swallow us up, and we prefer that it doesn't do that.

Roger and You

See what I mean about Bob? Here's a guy in a 5,000-square-foot store, 440 yards from a 120,000-square-foot Home Depot. Did he punt? Did he run for cover? Did he bitch and moan? No, he figured out ways to work over, around, through, and *with* Goliath.

When you're facing your Goliath, think of this story: For years, people thought it would be impossible to run a mile in less than four minutes. Then, in 1954, Roger Bannister ran it in 3 minutes and 59.4 seconds. Shortly thereafter, several other runners ran sub-four-minute miles, too.

Once something "impossible" has been done, it becomes attainable for many others. People like Bob Curry are the Roger Bannisters of business. You can be, too.

Notes

[1] Jeff Slutsky with Marc Slutsky, *StreetSmart Marketing* (New York: John Wiley & Sons, Inc., 1989), 1–2.

[2] Ibid., 13.

Part Four

Push the

Envelope

By now, the sight of your company logo makes your rivals bite their nails to the bone. You're ready for the expert course. Part IV teaches you how to push the envelope:

- Exploit every opportunity to torment your competition (Chapter 13, Carpe Diem).

- Ignore the rules of engagement—let's be honest, "rules of engagement" is an oxymoron anyway (Chapter 14, Draw Outside the Lines).

- Defeat the enemy when the enemy is someone you

work for (Chapter 15, How to Drive Your Boss Crazy).

- Defend the gains you've worked so hard to achieve (Chapter 16, Preserve and Protect).

Carpe Diem

Opportunities are seldom labeled.

John Shedd

The Hippies and the Doughboy

I n early 1984, a few months after the battle between Apple and IBM began with the introduction of Macintosh, another David-versus-Goliath war started in Burlington, Vermont. This war also involved a company started by two ex-hippies battling a *Fortune* 500 mega-company.

In his book, *Ben & Jerry's: The Inside Scoop*, Fred Lager explains that the conflict started in March 1984, when Ben Cohen, cofounder of the ice cream company, received a call from the company's distributor in

Boston. The distributor, Paul Tosi of Paul's Distributors, told Ben at a meeting the next day that Häagen-Dazs had threatened to stop selling ice cream to Paul's if it continued to sell Ben & Jerry's products.

Ben's reaction was to laugh at the outrageousness of Häagen-Dazs's ultimatum. First of all, the threat flew in the face of antitrust laws. Second, he couldn't believe that Häagen-Dazs considered Ben & Jerry's to be competition because Ben & Jerry's was selling only $4 million of ice cream per year at the time. Häagen-Dazs had a 70 percent market share and was part of the $4 billion Pillsbury Corporation.

One of the early decisions Ben & Jerry's made in response to the threat was to position the controversy as a battle between two hippies and a conglomerate, not as warfare between two ice cream companies. Häagen-Dazs handed Ben & Jerry's a golden opportunity to tell the world that its ice cream was *handcrafted* in Vermont while its competition's was *manufactured* by a huge conglomerate.

Ben & Jerry's sent out press releases declaring their intention to seek a restraining order and held two press conferences. While Ben met with a representative of the Federal Trade Commission, Jerry started a one-man picket in front of Pillsbury's headquarters in Minnesota. He held a hand-lettered sign that asked, "What's the Doughboy Afraid Of?" He passed out a leaflet that contained this message:

Do you think the Doughboy is afraid of two guys working with twenty-three people in four thousand square feet of rented space? Do you think the Doughboy is afraid he's only going to make $185.3 million in profits this year instead of $185.4 million? Do you think that maybe the Doughboy is afraid of the American Dream?

We only want to make our ice cream in Vermont and let the people of Boston and New England make their choice in the supermarket, where guys like us can compete with guys like the Doughboy. Next time you're in your local market, pick up a pint of Ben & Jerry's and give it a taste. Because to tell you the truth, *that's* what the Doughboy is really afraid of.

A coupon on the back of the flyer solicited orders for a Doughboy write-in kit. The kit contained pre-written protest letters to the FTC and the chairman of Pillsbury, pre-addressed envelopes, and a What's the Doughboy Afraid Of? bumper sticker. The Minnesota press wrote stories about

Jerry's picket. Associated Press picked up the story and spread it around the United States.

Ben & Jerry's also ran a $250 classified ad for supporters in *Rolling Stone* magazine, put up a billboard along Route 128 (the main arterial road to Boston), ran protest ads on the backs of buses, and had a plane tow a banner over a Boston College football game. It also placed a sticker on its ice cream containers with an 800 number for people to call for the Doughboy write-in kit.[1]

E x e r c i s e

Why do you think Häagen-Dazs didn't settle the lawsuit and avoid the bad publicity?

a. **Naïveté**

b. **Stupidity**

c. **Arrogance**

d. **Lousy legal advice**

e. **Häagen-Dazs management enjoyed depositions**

Grasp the Situation As It Really Is

The war between Ben & Jerry's and Häagen-Dazs illustrates the point of this chapter: Seize opportunities in unlikely places and use them to your advantage. Ben & Jerry's took what could have been a legal nightmare that broke the company and turned it into one of the greatest public relations coups in American business history.

More than fifteen thousand Doughboy write-in kits were sent out. Feature stories appeared in *The New York Times*, the *Wall Street Journal*, the *Boston Globe*, and the *San Francisco Chronicle*. By 1987 the war was settled between Häagen-Dazs and Ben & Jerry's. Häagen-Dazs was essentially barred from disrupting Ben & Jerry's distribution channel.

More important than a legal and business victory, however, was the public relations bonanza that Ben & Jerry's reaped. Hundreds of thousands of people who had never heard of Ben & Jerry's were wondering why Pillsbury was trying to restrain the company's ice cream.

Häagen-Dazs's actions weren't just about unfair business practices or the restraint of trade. They were an attack on entrepreneurship, motherhood, and apple pie, so Ben & Jerry's seized the moral high ground. The first step they took was to grasp the situation: Here was an opportunity, not just a threat, and they positioned the opportunity in the best possible way.

Develop Insights

Häagen-Dazs's threats provided Ben & Jerry's with a we-couldn't-have-designed-it-better-ourselves opportunity to garner publicity and support. However, Ben & Jerry's still had to develop the insight that Pillsbury would tarnish its wholesome, popping-fresh image by trying to squeeze two Vermont hippies out of business. The American public's love of entrepreneurs and underdogs is too powerful a tradition to accept this kind of heavy-handedness. Ben & Jerry's actions illustrate the second step of seizing the day: Develop insights into how to capitalize on a fortuitous situation.

Serve Your Competition's Customer

Häagen-Dazs's action was a once-in-a-lifetime opportunity for Ben & Jerry's. The more typical scenario for seizing the day is when your competition screws up, blinks, or drops the ball. When this occurs, ask yourself, "How can I serve my competition's customer?"

For example, much to the delight of Kiwi International, the airline mentioned earlier that makes every employee a salesperson, American Airlines went on strike during Thanksgiving in 1993. This strike presented Kiwi with the chance to be a white knight.

Maxine Krill, Kiwi's director of sales administration, went on the attack and sent over fifteen hundred faxes to travel agents in New York, Orlando, and San Juan announcing the availability of seats on Kiwi flights on routes affected by the strike.

According to Beth Mack, Kiwi's vice president of sales and marketing, "We asked ourselves, 'What can we do to take advantge of the situation and encourage people to choose Kiwi?'" In addition to the fax blitz, Kiwi put up signs at its counters that said "Welcome American Airlines passengers," and encouraged its personnel to acknowledge them personally.

Mack continues, "Passengers were scrambling for flights, and travel agents couldn't get through to American because all the lines were busy. Since the travel agent's responsibility is to accommodate the customer, we took the bull by the horns and basically said to agents, 'Don't forget about us.'"

E x e r c i s e

Suppose American Airlines sent a fax to travel agents when the strike was settled saying something to the effect of "We want to thank Kiwi for helping out our passengers during our strike. Things are back to normal now. We are offering the most flexible and complete schedule of flights with the most convenient gate connections."

What would have been the long-term effects of Kiwi's actions?

Like Kiwi, First Interstate Bank of California took advantage of the competition blinking to swipe customers. First Interstate's opportunity came when Security Pacific Bank announced it would merge with Bank of America. Soon thereafter, Bank of America started to close some of Security Pacific's offices.

Among other actions, trucks were dispatched to Security Pacific branches that were closing and became the white knight of the "abandoned" customers. Outside the Security Pacific branches, First Interstate employees urged customers to switch over to First Interstate and offered free checking for a year, free first-order checks, and other free services.

This self-proclaimed guerrilla marketing campaign was put into gear the day the merger was announced. First Interstate gained approximately

$1 billion in deposits for all its efforts. "This was a once-in-a-lifetime opportunity given the number of branches they were going to be closing," reports Dennis Shirley, senior vice president and marketing director of First Interstate.[2]

Look for Connections

Another way to develop insights is to look for connections, puns, or tie-ins that make $2 + 2 = 5$. For example, a few weeks before the 1993 major league baseball season, the San Francisco Giants were replacing a chain-link fence in the outfield of their stadium. Pat Gallagher, the senior vice president of business operations for the team, saw a connection for an advertising opportunity.

The areas to the left and right of centerfield are called, in baseball lingo, the gap. Coincidentally, Gap Inc., the clothing manufacturer and retailer, is a San Francisco–area company. One of its owners had also become a Giants limited partner during a recent ownership change.

Seizing the day, Gallagher pitched Gap on putting its sign in the two gaps in the outfield wall, and Gap went for it. Whenever a batter hit a ball deep into either side of the outfield, Gap signs appeared on television in front of thousands of viewers.

Any other company's ad in the gap would have been much less effective. It is the connection—the pun—that made Gap's signs in the gap a terrific advertisement that attracted a great deal of attention, such as radio announcers mentioning the signs during games.

Note: a corollary of seeing connections is to stash away a reserve in your marketing budget to take advantage of connections when you see them. Their serendipitous nature makes it difficult to plan for them in advance, but you should assume they will present themselves.

Squeeze the Trigger

After Ben & Jerry's appraised the situation and developed its insight into an opportunity, the company still needed the courage to sue a huge competitor. Pillsbury might very well have out-litigated Ben & Jerry's and "won" a protracted legal case even if it was morally or legally wrong.

Ben & Jerry's took its message to the highest court in the land: American public opinion. This was Ben & Jerry's way of squeezing the trigger. After you grasp your situation and develop insights, you still need the courage to fire the shot. Here are three examples to inspire you to take that final step.

Steal Your Competitor's Thunder

Software publisher Ashton-Tate stole its competition's thunder during the 1984 Summer Olympics. At the time Lotus Development Corporation was the dominant software company, and it secretly bought approximately $3 million of television spots to run during the Olympics.

Lotus was about to make a statement, "We are changing the rules of software marketing forever. If you want to play, you have to be big enough to pay." (Until then no software company had ever advertised on national television.)

An Ashton-Tate executive found out about Lotus's plans and went on the attack. He bought spots on the USA Network plus local spots before and after but not during Olympic coverage in several major U.S. cities. Then he announced that Ashton-Tate had produced the first national and Olympic coverage software advertisement for television (*national* because of the USA Network spots and *Olympic* because of the local spots adjacent to Olympic broadcasts).

The Ashton-Tate announcement came out before Lotus's ads ran, and Lotus, having been preempted, announced a week after Ashton-Tate that it too had a television campaign. Ashton-Tate's total cost was under $200,000—less than one tenth of Lotus's expenditures—and it got the thunder instead of Lotus.

Piggyback on Your Competition's Efforts

In 1986 British Airways ran a promotion that gave away 5,200 free flights for travel on June tenth of that year. It created a massive amount of awareness for British Airways—and also for Virgin Atlantic Airways, British Airways' competition.

173

Virgin Atlantic, spurred on by its advertising agency, Korey, Kay & Partners, piggybacked on British Airways' promotion by running this ad:

IT HAS ALWAYS BEEN VIRGIN'S POLICY TO ENCOURAGE YOU TO FLY TO LONDON FOR AS LITTLE AS POSSIBLE.

SO ON JUNE 10 WE ENCOURAGE YOU TO FLY BRITISH AIRWAYS.

As for the rest of the year, we look forward to seeing you aboard Virgin Atlantic. For the best service possible. At the lowest possible fare.

VIRGIN ATLANTIC AIRWAYS
Take us for all we've got.

Because of the ad, each time the news carried the story of British Airways' offer, there was also mention of Virgin Atlantic's response. British Airways' promotion cost millions of dollars in free seats; Virgin Atlantic's cost a few ads.

By piggybacking on its competitor's efforts, Virgin Atlantic was able to neutralize a competitor's attack and turn it into publicity for itself.

Look for—and Embrace—Gifts

When you're handed a gift, embrace it and hope your competition doesn't get the same gift. This is the lesson of Paper Direct, a mail-order paper company in Secaucus, New Jersey, whose customers seem to like to design new products for it.

It started in 1989 when Paper Direct ran sidebars in its catalog showing how customers were using its products. "Whenever we did focus groups, customers told us they loved seeing what other people were doing," says vice president of sales Rick Schwartz.

Paper Direct seized this opportunity by sponsoring a nationwide "Show Us Your Stuff" contest for customers to show how they used Paper Direct's stationery, envelopes, and specialty papers. The customer who displayed the most creative design won $500 in Paper Direct goods.

Because of the contest, Paper Direct saw that some customers were modifying and customizing paper—giving Paper Direct new product ideas. "We got a lot of suggestions and new product ideas through the contest," says Schwartz. "They were taking our products and adding new twists." New-product ideas are hard enough to come up with, so why not get them for free?

Create Your Own Day

One step beyond seizing the day is creating your own day—that is, causing or catalyzing something worth seizing. For example, Levi Strauss & Co., the San Francisco–based clothing manufacturer, commissioned a study on wearing casual clothes in the workplace.

A research company surveyed 750 white-collar workers around the United States. The company found that 81 percent of the people believed casual dress improves morale, 47 percent believed it increases productivity, and only 4 percent thought it would have a negative impact. Forty-six percent also said they would consider casual dress an attraction to going to work for a company.

When Levi Strauss obtained these results, the company went on a public relations blitz that resulted in newspaper and magazine stories extolling the virtues of casual dress. Levi Strauss, not coincidentally, would be one of the largest benefactors of greater acceptance of casual dress in the workplace because it manufactures a line of casual clothes called Dockers.

Levi Strauss was in a no-lose position. If the results of the poll were positive, then it would publicize it. If the results were negative, then it would bury it—they commissioned the study, so they could do anything they wanted with it. Then, in true drive-your-competition-crazy mode, Levi Strauss implemented a toll-free hotline that offered advice on adopting casual dress standards.*

The study generated three thousand news stories, and Levi Strauss further capitalized on interest in the trend by creating for human-resources managers a kit that offered advice on implementing a casual-wear program, complete with case studies of how other companies implemented their programs. Brilliant. Just brilliant.

E x e r c i s e

Suppose Exxon commissioned a study and found that damage from the Exxon *Valdez* spill had been completely reversed and that conditions were better than they had been before the oil spill.

Who would believe this study?

a. **The CEO of Exxon**

b. **The CEO and the executive staff**

c. **The CEO, the executive staff, and the PR firm that came up with the idea**

d. **The Environmental Protection Agency**

This technique requires two preconditions: First, you must have a positive public image. Levi could get away with commissioning and

*Try calling 1-800-DOCKERS.

publicizing the study because it has a progressive image. Use this rule of thumb: If a popular company does this, it's clever. If an unpopular company does this, it's manipulative.

Second, the findings of the report must be believable. Evidence supporting a preposterous notion shouldn't be used—even if the evidence is valid. It feels right, for example, that many businesspeople would support more casual dress in the contemporary environment of many industries.

Notes

[1]Fred Lager, *Ben & Jerry's: The Inside Scoop* (New York: Crown Publishers, Inc., 1994), 106–20.

[2]Teresa J. Gaines, "Guerrilla banking: First Interstate raids enemy territory for customers," *San Bernardino County Sun*, 3 August 1993, B8.

Chapter 14

Draw Outside the Lines

**The things that haven't been done before
Are the tasks worthwhile today;
Are you one of the flock that follows, or
Are you one that shall lead the way
Are you one of the timid souls that quail
At the jeers of a doubting crew,
Or dare you, whether you win or fail,
Strike out for a goal that's new?**

Edgar Guest

On April 19, 1775, British troops marched toward Concord, Massachusetts, to destroy the military stores of the American revolutionaries. On the first day of battle, the British and American forces fought on an open, flat area called Lexington Green.

The British and the Americans both used the conventional fighting style of the time: lining up in tight, closed ranks and firing upon each other. The British forces quickly prevailed and forced the Americans to disperse.

Later the same day the Americans changed their tactics as the British returned to Boston. This time, instead of firing in close ranks as dictated by tradition, the Americans attacked from bushes on the sides of the road. This time the Americans took a heavy toll on the British.

Two battles were fought on the same day between the same opponents. One battle was fought within the lines—according to the traditional rules of engagement. The other battle was fought outside the lines, and the side that broke the rules achieved success.

According to Robert Asprey in *War in the Shadows*, a British general warned his country of Americans and American tactics:

> Composed as the American army is, together with the strength of the country, full of wood, swamps, stone walls, and other inclosures and hiding places, it may be said of it that every private man will in action be his own general, who will turn every tree and bush into a kind of temporary fortress, from whence, when he hath fired his shot with all the deliberation, coolness, and uncertainty which hidden safety inspires, he will skip as it were to the next, and so on for a long time till dislodged either by cannon or by a resolute attack of light infantry.[1]

Wouldn't you like your competition to say the same thing about you? It might if you have the courage to break the shackles that hold you down and draw outside the lines.

Connect the Dots

There are ethics, there are laws, and there is good taste, but there are few rules you cannot break to get ahead of your competition. The message of this chapter is to break tradition and use courage and imagination. John Czepiel, the author of *Competitive Marketing Strategy*, explains the situation perfectly: "Fight fair, but avoid fair fights."[2]

Don't let assumptions, conventions, and traditions hold you back or cloud your thinking. Anyone who's read a business book in the past ten years has probably seen the puzzle of connecting nine dots by using at most four lines and without lifting the pencil off the paper.

The conventional solution—well known now that this puzzle has appeared in so many books—is to throw out the assumption that you cannot draw outside of the dots and solve the puzzle as shown:[3]

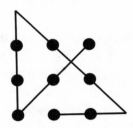

A less conventional but still well-known solution is to not assume that you must draw the lines through the center of each dot. Then it is possible to solve the puzzle this way:[4]

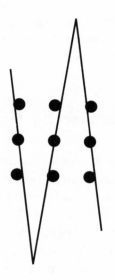

I want you to go beyond even these types of solutions. For example, if you really pushed the envelope, you could take a very large pencil and solve the puzzle this way:[5]

Finally, no one said that folding the paper to bring the dots close to one another and connectable with one line was prohibited.[6] Whether solving puzzles or driving the competition crazy, convention, sacred cows, and acculturation are the prisons from which we seek parole.

Be An Outsider or Act Like One

In case after case in American business history, outsiders have driven insiders crazy. Take, for example, the business of putting words on paper. At first, companies like Remington, Royal, Smith, and Underwood dominated the market with their mechanical typewriters. Later an outsider, IBM, came and stole the market from them with its electric typewriters. Then, new outsiders like Wang decimated the typewriter industry with dedicated word-processing machines. Finally, outsider Apple Computer, and eventually IBM, made dedicated word processors obsolete with personal computers running word-processing software.

James M. Utterback, a professor of management and engineering at MIT, explains in his book, *Mastering the Dynamics of Innovation*, how outsiders achieve these kinds of results:

Industry outsiders have little to lose in pursuing radical innovations. They have no infrastructure of existing technology to defend or maintain and ... they have every economic incentive to overturn the existing order.

Industry insiders, on the other hand, have abundant reasons to be slow to mobilize in developing radical innovations. Economically, they have huge investments in the current technology; emotionally, they and their fortunes are heavily bound up in the status quo; and from a practical point of view, their managerial attention is encumbered by the system they have—just maintaining and marginally improving their existing systems is a full-time occupation.[7]

If you are an outsider, use Utterback's wisdom as empowerment to draw outside the lines: pursue radical innovations and overturn the existing order. If you are an insider, use Utterback's wisdom to goad you into acting like an outsider, because if you don't overturn the existing order, someone else will. First, let's see how to ignore convention.

Ignore Convention

Pity the poor echidna. Captain William Bligh documented this animal's existence on a voyage to Australia in 1793. (This was a trip Bligh and a small number of loyal crewmen had taken after having been "rightsized" from the *Bounty*.) The echidna is an egg-laying anteater that combines reptilian and mammalian characteristics like its relative the duck-billed platypus.[8]

Because it exhibited reptilian characteristics such as laying eggs, biologists in the early 1800s typecast the echidna as primitive—not quite up to the standards of us mammals. These biologists ignored one minor detail: the echidna has a very large brain for its body size.

We can surmise that these biologists cherished their precious theory: reptilian equals primitiveness. This theory was so powerful that it prevented them from seeing an obvious and myth-shattering fact: the echidna's big head. Retrofitting a popular riddle, we might ask, "Which came first—the brain or the egg?" The answer for biologists in the 1800s was clearly the egg.

Like these biologists, businesspeople can become prisoners of conventional wisdom, traditional methods, and the holiest of mismanagement litanies: "This is the way things have always been done." My message: Resist the known and defend the unknown. Switching from biology to business, here are examples of how companies have done this.

Exercise

True or false? Managers would rather delegate problems that cannot be solved than empower subordinates to implement solutions that cannot be understood.

Conventional Wisdom

Bank One Columbus N.A. of Columbus, Ohio, and the American Association of Retired People (AARP) of Washington, D.C., have worked together to provide credit cards to senior citizens. An action that Bank One has taken is to approve credit to senior citizens based on their net worth rather than their previous credit history or current income.[9]

This policy helps widows who don't have their own credit standing. According to Debbie Salerno, the Bank One vice president in charge of the program, "They have a lower delinquency rate than the industry average, and they are more likely to pay on their account because it's their only credit card. Other companies would not grant them cards because they didn't have a credit record established in their name. They're very loyal and responsible."

By ignoring the conventional wisdom, Bank One opened a new market and enhanced its image among senior citizens. If you think about it for ten seconds, it becomes obvious that credit based on net worth makes sense for these customers.

Bank One's policy yields two lessons. First, it reiterates the lessons of Chapter 5, "Focus on Your Customers." The traditional method of credit analysis puts the customer second, not first. The first consideration is the need of the financial institution to get repaid. This is the wrong order if you want to drive your competition crazy. You'll usually find that ignoring conventional wisdom is as easy as placing your customer's needs ahead of yours.

Second, this example illustrates the relationship of convention and intuition. Allow me to draw outside the lines of business examples, and cite Jack E. Oliver, a professor of geology at Cornell University:

The trick is to break with convention, not necessarily with intuition. Most new discoveries are not so much counter to good intuition as they are counter to "conventional wisdom" of the science at the time.[10]

Conventional Practice

The Electronic Scriptorium is a Virginia-based firm that automates libraries, publishes CD-ROMs, develops software, and provides data-entry services. Ed Leonard, founder of the company, discovered a highly educated, highly disciplined group of workers with impeccable personal habits: monks.[11]

Leonard contracts projects to monks from six monasteries across the country. According to Leonard,

All the work is done right inside the monasteries. The quality of their work is exceptionally high because the monks are not distracted by many of the things the average worker is. The monastic training teaches them that the monastery is a holy place; the equipment is viewed as an extension of the monastery, so they treat it with respect and honor.

Leonard developed a new solution to his problem of finding a stable workforce, because he defined his needs in terms of a dependable workforce instead of the conventional practice of hiring data-entry clerks. When you stop paying homage to conventional practices, you can uncover solutions that will leave your competition asking, "Why didn't we think of that?"

Conventional Perspectives

Usually warranty and service obligations are seen as profit-eroding nuisances. For example, California law requires a one-year warranty on labor for building contractors. Most contractors consider this an onerous burden that can eat up profits, but one California firm turned this obligation into a weapon to generate more business.

This company installs roofs, gutters, insulation, and other residential products. An employee calls every customer eleven months after installation to ask if he or she needs any repairs while the work is still under warranty. The calls generate a small amount of warranty work and a huge amount of new work and referrals.[12]

A second California plumbing, electrical, heating, and air-conditioning company boosted sales 15 to 30 percent when it turned customer complaints into an opportunity.

The company charges a minimum of one hour's labor for service calls. Customers complained that technicians often finished their job and left after thirty or forty minutes. Now technicians explain what was done and why and then tell the customer they have a certain amount of time remaining in their hour. Technicians then ask, "Is there anything you'd like me to check while I'm here?"

This simple question often generates work beyond the one-hour minimum, and the company gains business simply because it ignored the conventional perspective that "a minimum is a minimum."[13]

E x e r c i s e

When your customer's warranty period is about to expire, you

a. Breathe a sigh of relief

b. Count the days

c. Contact the customer to see if there's anything you can do

---

Conventional Distribution

Odwalla juice is as close to freshly squeezed as it gets. The company uses no preservatives, and its juices stay fresh in stores because supplies are restocked every day by Odwalla's salespeople who visit retailers in a company-owned fleet of trucks.

Perhaps making your deliveries with your own salesforce is a big molehill (large companies like Frito Lay and Coca-Cola are traditionally the only kinds of food businesses that utilize fleets of company trucks), but according to Brian Lovejoy, Odwalla's director of marketing, it's worth it. Odwalla drives the competition crazy by handling their own product from manufacturer to in-store display in Odwalla's coolers.

Says Lovejoy, "Our competitors don't have such control on the shelf. They rely on the stores to stock and display their products. By controlling shelf space, we can merchandize exactly the way we want. If someone else is stocking your product for you, you can't." By eliminating the middlemen, Odwalla has taken control of its own fate.

Bend the Rules

A nother way to draw outside the lines is to bend the rules of the game. When I was first hired by Apple, Mike Murray, the director of marketing for the Macintosh Division, told me he wanted the best collection of software for a personal computer. Ever. He didn't care how I did it, and he didn't want me to claim I failed because I played by the rules.

Given this charter, or more accurately, intimidated by this charter, we set off to bend rules and get Macintosh software. For example, Apple corporate (as opposed to the Macintosh Division) operated a program for professional software developers that included the ability to buy hardware for programming at a 50 percent discount. At the time, this discount was the largest offered to any channel. To be admitted to the program, developers had to prove that they were really in the software business by submitting business plans, examples of current products, and other superfluous pieces of evidence. The intent of this practice was to prevent people from subverting the dealer channel.

One of the first actions I took was to lower the fence to join this program. I preapproved applications for Macintosh developers, and I ignored the fact that people didn't have a "company" per se. All I cared about was that they expressed an interest in writing software. If they were bending the truth, so be it. Better to let a few folks defeat the system and get good prices than turn away a single sincere developer.

One of the rules of the developer program was that a company could only buy five or so computers of each model per year. The intent of this rule was to prevent companies from buying computers for nonprogramming staff as well as for friends, relatives, and other outsiders. Again, Apple was trying to protect its dealers.

Again, I bent rules. I let companies buy as many Macintoshes as they wanted. Did Macintoshes get in the hands of people through this program that they shouldn't have? Absolutely. Did it matter? Only in a positive sense, for two reasons: first, if I was cajoling developers to create as much Macintosh software as possible as quickly as possible, how could I enforce a rule that limited their access to more Macintoshes? Second, on a broader front, I believed that each Macintosh being used by *anyone*—much less a developer—would sell more Macintoshes, so I looked the other way.

I bent the rules one other time. After a year of hounding software developers and achieving results, we still faced a problem with our own salesforce, which didn't believe that software was really shipping. Murray told me to think of a way to convince the Apple field salespeople that Macintosh software was shipping. My solution was to buy $750,000 worth of newly completed Macintosh software from companies and distribute samples to the field salespeople and dealers.

Unfortunately, this exceeded my spending authority by $745,000, so the controller of the Macintosh Division wanted to fire me. Only John Sculley, then president of Apple, had a spending authority of this size. Murray interceded on my behalf and explained the reason for this expenditure.

My personal experience in bending rules enables me to provide these tips:

- Know thy boss and thy boss's boss. I knew that Murray would support my efforts and that his boss, Steve Jobs, would, too. Steve was cofounder and chairman of the company. He could protect me for bending the rules if it came down to that. (He would also fire me if I didn't deliver the software.)

- Know thy company. In some companies, no matter who your boss and your boss's boss are, you can't get away with bending the rules. Apple is a company where you can, but not every company is like Apple.

- Even if your boss, your boss's boss, and the company will tolerate your actions, ask yourself if your actions are ethical and legal. You could be just working for a bunch of crooks, and you are all caught up in ends-justifies-the-means *meshugas*.

■ Ask yourself what you would do if someone working for you did what you are thinking of doing. Would you smile or laugh and think the person is clever? Then it's probably okay. Would you get angry and think the person is unethical? Then it's probably not.

■ Ask yourself if the parties that might be harmed by your rule-bending would sanction your actions if they understood all the consequences. For example, Apple dealers would probably condone my developer program rule-bending since greater availability of Macintosh software meant they could sell more Macintoshes.

In most cases of drawing outside the lines, someone had the courage and audacity (or naïveté) to try something without either explicit permission or explicit prohibition. But make sure your actions are implicitly ethical, whether specifically prohibited or not.

Let a Thousand Flowers Bloom

Another example of bending the rules comes to us from Chattanooga, Tennessee. Here a law prohibits companies from having more than one free-standing sign that advertises the business. Goodyear store service manager Darrell Smith figured out a way to bend this law in May 1994.

Since Smith's facility already had one sign, he spelled out "Goodyear" in marigolds. Passersby could read the sign because the flower bed was on a fifteen-degree slope. The store didn't have two signs—it had one sign and one flower garden. One city inspector considered this a violation, but the public rallied behind Smith, and the municipal government backed off.[14]

The key to getting away with this method of drawing outside the lines is to be clever. Creating a sign that skirts the law is not enough. Cleverness is everything—in Smith's case, his "sign" was so ingenious that citizens rallied around him.

Stuff the Ballot Box

Each year *Macworld* magazine sponsors a contest called the World Class Awards. Readers are asked to vote for their favorite products in categories such as database, word processor, and graphics. As president of a small, upstart Macintosh software company after I left Apple, I sent letters and even furnished a ballot to our customers asking them to vote for our product.

Microsoft, the $10 billion start-up in Washington, protested my actions. (Note: This is the same company that was investigated by the Federal Trade Commission for antitrust violations.) In my mind, asking our users to vote for our product was no different from political parties registering people to vote. In Microsoft's mind, there was a rule against encouraging people to vote for a product.

We won the award, but "stuffing" the ballot box was more fun. Our actions did not involve falsifying ballots from fictitious people. We simply encouraged our own customers to vote for our product—mobilizing a group of satisfied users. It's not my fault that Microsoft didn't think of this.

Fly the Unfriendly Skies

When other radio stations have exclusive rights to cover a San Francisco Bay Area event, radio station KFRC makes its presence known by attaching a ninety-by-twenty-foot banner with the KFRC logo to a plane and flying it over the crowds.

According to marketing director Mark Arnold, "It's just so huge, there's no way you could miss it. What are competitors going to do—shoot down the plane?" KFRC is piggybacking on the efforts of its competitors.

A guerrilla technique? Absolutely. Clever? Yes. Tacky? Slightly. The reason KFRC's action isn't too unethical is that "exclusive coverage" refers to who is broadcasting the event, not flying over it with a plane. If KFRC snuck into the event and started broadcasting the event, too, then it would be acting unethically.

E x e r c i s e

True or false? Nike was an official sponsor of the 1992 Summer Olympics.

(Answer: False. Nike wasn't, but you'd be hard-pressed to know this. Not being an official sponsor saved Nike $30 million.[15])

Play with Their Minds

The final way to draw outside the lines is to play with the minds of your competition. I am not advocating lying. Lying is when you tell people things that are not true. Playing with your competition's mind is when you encourage it to reach an incorrect conclusion by itself.

These actions by themselves seldom help you serve your customer better or increase sales, but they are fun, and having fun is a legitimate business goal. They also relieve stress, and relieving stress is a legitimate business function. Finally, they can help to unnerve your competition and knock it off balance.

In 1988 as president of a Macintosh software start-up company, I battled then-industry-giant Ashton-Tate and had a wonderful time playing with its employees' minds. At the time, Ashton-Tate had sales revenues of $250 million with more than one thousand employees, and our company had $750,000 of capital and twenty employees. Our product was called 4th Dimension, and the Ashton-Tate product was called dBase Mac.

The Ashton-Tate product manager of dBase Mac bought a copy of 4th Dimension and registered in our database of owners—obviously, he was trying to know thy enemy. (I don't remember if we figured out he was in our registered-user database because we were so smart or because the database was so small.)

I sent the fellow a company coffee mug as if all customers were getting one. A cover letter explained that we were so successful that we were giving mugs to our customers to thank them for their support. (The letter didn't say *all* customers were getting a mug.)

Unfortunately, Ashton-Tate didn't go out and spend thousands of dollars on mugs for its customers. So did my deed accomplish anything positive? Probably not, but I bet it made the product manager think twice about our commitment to customer relations. Did it help our customers? Certainly not. But my employees and I had a good laugh doing it. And, like I said above, having fun is a legitimate goal.

(Note: If you do something similar, and the competition ratchets up service in response and makes your life more difficult, don't blame me.)

In case you need greater inspiration, here are five more examples:

- An electrician who had only one truck was razzed by his buddies (they were not, strictly speaking, his competition) that he didn't have a fleet of trucks. To fake them out, on the right side of his truck he painted #3, on the left #4, and on the back #5.[16]

- Dan Eilers, president and chief executive officer of Claris Corporation, had his company cut a great deal for ClarisWorks with schools in the suburbs surrounding Microsoft. Was he concerned with the quality of education in these areas? Not especially, but ClarisWorks competes with Microsoft Works, and he wanted the kids of Microsoft employees to tell their parents they were using the Claris product.

- During the Korean War, the Office of Strategic Services left behind a cache of supplies for the Communist Chinese to find. One of the items was a box of specially manufactured, extra-large condoms labeled MADE IN THE USA SIZE MEDIUM.[17]

- When Hannibal was fighting the Romans in 217 B.C., he was lured into an ambush by General Fabius. Hannibal had his troops tie bundles of brushwood to the horns of two thousand cattle, light the bundles at night, and march the cattle toward the Romans. In the ensuing confusion, Hannibal and his troops escaped the ambush.[18]

- A truckers' strike threatened to shut down the International Harvester factory in Melrose Park, Illinois, because steel could not be delivered to the plant. The strike was enforced by snipers who would shoot at trucks that were trying to defy it. Workers from International Harvester rented school buses and dressed as nuns. They loaded the steel on the buses and delivered it. Who would shoot at school buses driven by nuns?[19]

The Greatest Story Ever Told

You may not have a fleet of trucks, big condoms, a herd of cattle, or drivers dressed as nuns, but sometimes you can still drive your competition crazy by simply leading them astray. This chapter ends with the greatest story I've ever heard about playing with your competition's mind.

In the early sixties Wilson Harrel purchased a cleaning solution called Formula 409 and began retailing it. By 1967 he had acquired a 5 percent share of the U.S. cleaning-products market; unfortunately, it was at this point that gigantic Procter & Gamble began test-marketing its liquid cleaner, Cinch.

Harrel discovered that Procter & Gamble's first test market was Denver, Colorado. Harrel withdrew Formula 409 from the Denver market by discouraging reorders from stores, and to further dampen sales he stopped advertising and promoting the product there.

Naturally, his actions resulted in phenomenal results for Cinch in the area, and Procter & Gamble implemented a national launch since the Denver test had "proven" that an investment in Cinch was worthwhile.

Having boosted Procter & Gamble's expectations for Cinch, Harrel set out to destroy its national introduction. He bundled the sixteen-ounce size of Formula 409 and the half-gallon size and sold the two for $1.48

retail—a huge discount for both products. He figured that most consumers who bought this bundle wouldn't have to buy a cleaning product for six months.

Harrel heavily advertised and promoted this low-priced special—effectively taking Formula 409 users out of the market. The only customers left for Cinch were new users, but there weren't enough to justify Procter & Gamble's huge investment. In less than a year, Procter & Gamble removed Cinch from the shelves.[20]

What are the lessons here?

- Know thy enemy! Harrel's knowledge of how Procter & Gamble test-markets a product before rolling it out nationally enabled him to outfox the giant.

- But you don't need to know much. Anyone who reads business magazines or business books could figure out Procter & Gamble's *modus operandi*. We're not talking deep-throat, deceptive, high-tech, clandestine spying here.

- There's no such thing as a cinch, so don't let vanity and arrogance cloud your thinking. Surely someone in Procter & Gamble should have noticed what Harrel was doing.

Interview: Stephen Wynn

If you've ever been to a hotel that Stephen Wynn created, you'd remember it. The Mirage in Las Vegas, for example, features a volcano that erupts every few minutes. The registration area contains a twenty-thousand-gallon aquarium with sharks and stingrays. There's also a 1.5-million-gallon Dolphin Habitat as well as a display of the Royal White tigers that are used in the Siegfried and Roy show at the hotel.

Next door to the Mirage is another Wynn hotel: Treasure Island. This hotel's design was inspired by the Robert Louis Stevenson novel. Its entrance features an hourly battle between the pirate ship *Hispaniola* and the British frigate HMS *Britannia*, and one ship actually sinks. Treasure Island is also home to the French-Canadian performing troupe Cirque du Soleil.

Wynn is the chairman of the board and chief executive officer of Mirage Resorts International. His company owns the Mirage, Treasure Island, Golden Nugget Las Vegas, and Golden Nugget Laughlin, and it is building another hotel in Las Vegas called Beau Rivage. (A man-made lake large enough for waterskiing will surround this hotel.)

Las Vegas is changing—or, perhaps more accurately, Wynn is changing Las Vegas. It used to be a town that catered to interests of adults. Now it is focusing more and more on families who come not to *gamble* but to *vacation*. Wynn's hotels are leading the charge of this trend.

Most people consider Wynn a swashbuckling entrepreneur who draws outside the lines with bold abandon. In this interview, however, he moderates this image and offers sage advice about when and how to be different. The goal, after all, of companies is to please customers and make money, not to be different for the sake of being different.

Q: The press credits you with breaking all the rules of casino gambling and "reinventing" Las Vegas. Is this accurate?

I haven't changed the rules. I've just intensified the things that were here before. Caesar's Palace is the breakaway property in the history of Las Vegas. Jay Sarno came here in the mid-sixties and built it. Up to that time, the hotels were all the same: a hotel from the fifties with a casino in front of it and a showroom.

Sarno created a whole new environment from the costumes to the names of the restaurants to the interior decorating that had the theme of a bacchanalian feast. Jay's theory was that the entire place—not just the showroom—ought to be the entertainment, so walking around ought to be a fanciful experience.

My idea was that if I could create a tropical, South Pacific, Polynesian-looking lagoon in the middle of the harsh and inhospitable Las Vegas desert, people would see something with their eyes that their minds would tell them should not be there. The tension between what they're seeing and what they're supposed to be seeing would be so fetching that it would be irresistible and make them ask, "Could the inside of this place be as outrageous as the outside? Let's go find out."

194

Q: But didn't you once break the unwritten rule of Las Vegas that "Thou shalt not take on Caesar's Palace"?

We built a restaurant at the Golden Nugget, which was the first gourmet room downtown. We took a picture of the room with the maitre d' standing in the foreground holding this beautiful platter of garnish in front of him. We put up a billboard on the freeway right behind Caesar's that said CAESAR'S PALACE, EAT YOUR HEART OUT.

The humor was that the Golden Nugget was challenging Caesar's Palace. It was like sticking your tongue out at the big guy, but I've found that defining ourselves with regard to another hotel is okay for a quick chuckle. Our success, however, is completely determined by the energy we apply to our own affairs. That is to say, we compete with ourselves.

Every single thing that we do—and every good thing that happens to us—happens because of what we do in our own building. It's not a poker game. A good poker player has to know the other guy's cards so he can play his right. In my business, it's entirely how you play your own cards. It doesn't matter what anybody else is doing.

Q: But can't you ignore the rules and make your own?

You cannot ignore the fundamentals. There are touchstones and walls. There are sides to the arena, and those sides are determined by who the customers are and what they want. People from all over the world come to Las Vegas because of Las Vegas's image as a party place.

You are successful to the extent that you give the people what they want. These are the fundamental rules. You toy with those babies, and you're a dead duck. I don't want you to think there is a tabula rasa. There's a lot of discipline to this.

Now, if you can be clever and resourceful and original in meeting that expectation, then you are creative, but you've got to meet people's expectation. Am I paying attention to the rules? That is the way we look at it. We just did a *better* job of paying attention to the rules.

Q: How do you know which rules, conventions, and walls you cannot break?

It boils down to fundamental common sense. In every situation, there are always fundamentals that must be observed. Creativity is not defined by your ability to throw convention entirely out of the window. That's just reckless foolishness. That's the earmark of a half-baked brain that says, "If I'm different, I'm original." You're just different.

Original and creative is to learn how to reexpress in new and unique ways the fundamentals that hold things together. For every place and for every time and for every situation, there are fundamentals, and they're determined by things as straightforward as consideration for other people.

People go to a place. They shop at a store. They need a product. Why do they need a product? They need the product because of a personal need. Every time I hear someone say "Let's break all the rules," unless it's someone doing it for dramatic effect, I know that I'm talking to a fool.

Q: If you're successful, pretty soon you are the old standard—the Caesar's Palace—and you've got to eat your own shorts or another Steve Wynn is going to eat them for you. How do you get out of your own status quo?

You just said it. Play back your tape: Either someone does it to you or you do it to yourself.

On February twenty-eighth, we're closing six hundred rooms—20 percent of our inventory—and we'll rotate 20 percent of the rooms every day until August twenty-fourth. We are spending $54 million to redo the hallways, rooms, and elevator lobby. Then we're going to redo every restaurant, so that by January of 1996, the Mirage is a new hotel. Although this is only our sixth year, we think we know exactly how to take care of this property.

Q: Which is?

Keep making it better and better and better. And then we're going to build another hotel, the Beau Rivage, where the Dunes was. It's going to be the most romantic hotel that's ever been built.

Q: So you'd rather cannibalize yourself?

Hopefully, I'm not going to cannibalize myself. We've got a hotel in Laughlin that has a room rate in the high twenties. We've got one downtown in the high fifties. We've got one next door in the high seventies. We've got one here in the high one hundred twenties. We've got one in every category. Now there's room for one at around $200. It's going to be like a Four Seasons. You don't cannibalize yourself if you create something new.

Q: Is there a volcano in front of this one?

No, this is something else. It's on an island. It's a different product.

Q: Final question: what's the role of competition?

Don't worry about the competition. Ignore them. Focus on the customer. Make an imaginative excursion into the mind of the customer. The more perfectly you can do that, the easier it will be for you to draw conclusions about what their reactions will be.

The next thing is a little tougher: you have to be creative enough or intuitive enough to come up with a new idea that will titillate them within the given framework. That's where the creativity comes in. That's where you get original.

"Creativity and originality" are such dangerous words. There have never been words that have been more abused, twisted, and bent than creativity and originality because they get substituted so often for just being different. Being different isn't tricky at all. Any fool can be different.

Notes

[1]Robert Asprey, *War in the Shadows* (New York: William Morrow and Company, Inc., 1994), 60–61.

[2]John Czepiel, *Competitive Marketing Strategy* (Englewood Cliffs, N.J.: Prentice Hall, 1992), 4.

[3]Don Reynolds, Jr., *How to Sharpen Your Competitive Edge* (Naperville, Ill.: Sourcebooks, Inc., 1994), 8.

[4]Michael Michalko, *Thinkertoys* (Berkeley: Ten Speed Press, 1991), 44.

[5]Reynolds, *How to Sharpen Your Competitive Edge*, 8.

[6]Ibid.

[7]James M. Utterback, *Mastering the Dynamics of Innovation* (Boston: Harvard Business School Press, 1994), 161–62.

[8]Stephen Jay Gould, *Bully for Brontosaurus: Reflections in Natural History* (New York: W. W. Norton & Company, 1991), 281–93.

[9]Judith Graham, "Seniors offered banking-at-home," *Advertising Age*, 13 June 1988, 30.

[10]Jack E. Oliver, *The Incomplete Guide to the Art of Discovery* (New York: Columbia University Press, 1991), 52.

[11]Jyoti Thottem, "Entrepreneur Finds Monks Make Heavenly Employees: Small Data-Services Firm Says Customers Are Flocking to Its Door," *Wall Street Journal*, 12 July 1993, sec. 8.

[12]Michael LeBoeuf, *Fast Forward* (New York: G.P. Putnam, 1994), 84.

[13]Ibid., 84–85.

[14]Bob Garfield, "Chattanooga Flower Sign Uproar," *All Things Considered*, National Public Radio, 31 March 1994.

[15]Donald Katz, *Just Do It* (New York: Random House, 1994), 36.

[16]Jeff Slutsky with Marc Slutsky, *StreetSmart Marketing* (New York: John Wiley & Sons, Inc., 1989), 14–15.

[17]From a 7/27/94 telephone interview with John Quinn of Quinn Associates, a company that does business intelligence and competitive intelligence work.

[18]Gottfried Schädlich, *Kriegslist gestern und heute (Tricks of War, Yesterday and Today)*, 2d ed. (Herford/Bonn, 1979). As cited in Harro Von Senger, *The Book of Stratagems* (New York: Penguin Books, 1991), 90.

[19]Jack Stack, *The Great Game of Business* (New York: Doubleday Currency, 1992), 27–28.

[20]Paul Solman and Thomas Friedman, *Life and Death on the Corporate Battlefield* (New York: Simon and Schuster, 1982), 25–27.

Chapter 15

How to Drive Your Boss Crazy

The cream rises until it sours.

Laurence Peter

Smell the Secondhand Smoke

The underlying assumption of this book is that your competition is another company or organization. However, this may not always be true. Your competition could be the person you work for.

Ideally, this chapter should not be necessary. Companies should have a clearly articulated mission supported by objectives, strategies, and tactics that will enable the company to achieve this mission. Then, because of ability, perseverance, skills, and timing, a few people should rise to management positions. Then, they should enable their employees to implement the company's objectives and to satisfy their needs for achievement, social interaction, and money.

Helllllooo? Wake up and smell the secondhand smoke. The world doesn't work this way, and bosses, unfortunately, can be as much of an opponent as the competition. On the other hand, if you have a good relationship with your boss—he* is effective, communicative, and empowering—then you can skip this chapter.

There comes a time in every employee's career when he or she must ask not what he or she can do for his or her boss, but what his or her boss can do for him or her.† If the answer keeps coming up "nothing," then it's time to make some changes. This chapter explains how.

Know Thy Boss

The first step is to know thy enemy—in this case, your boss. A lousy boss is usually a simple beast. His style can be described by seven general types. This is not to say that there are seven kinds of lousy bosses. Instead, a lousy boss usually exhibits characteristics of several of these styles. Also, over time, boss style can change, so you need to be prepared for all contingencies.

The Technodweeb

The Technodweeb relates better to a computer or mechanical device than he does to humans. Usually the Technodweeb rose through the engineering ranks because of his technical prowess. If he set his mind to it, he could probably be a decent manager—unfortunately, machines are more interesting to him than people. If he has lots of electrical power

---

*I use the male forms of pronouns in this chapter. I am neither stupid nor a male chauvinist pig (is there a difference?). Using dual pronouns, in my opinion, creates awkward writing. Also, most lousy bosses are male, so I am statistically correct. If this upsets you terribly, then I hope it's the worst thing that has happened in your life.
†See what I mean about pronouns?

outlets, he's a happy camper. (If this describes your boss, maybe you should see what you can do to increase the number of power outlets in his office.)

The Peter

Everyone knows that a star salesperson doesn't make a great sales manager. The trouble is, the star salesperson is still promoted to the management position because everyone thinks the Peter Principle ("In a hierarchy, every employee tends to rise to his level of incompetence") applies only to other companies. The problem with working for Peter is he's petered out and can't handle his present position, much less future challenges. No boss in the history of mankind has ever asked for a demotion.

The Boy Wonder

The Boy Wonder is a younger brother of Peter. Peter isn't self-confident—deep down inside he knows he's beyond his ability. The Boy Wonder, on the other hand, has the arrogant self-confidence of someone who hasn't been tested. The Boy Wonder may start out like a breath of fresh air, but even fresh air is unbearable when it's blowing hard enough. As a rule of thumb, no one under thirty years old should manage anyone.

The Company Man

The Company Man is where he is because he has outlasted everyone else. He isn't better or brighter than his peers—he's just more steadfast. Problems occur when he finally arrives in a place of power: he's least likely to embrace innovation and change. After all, innovation and change didn't get him to where he is. His justification for everything is "This is how it's always been done."

The Schmexpert

The Schmexpert is half schmuck and half expert. He knows enough jargon to be dangerous but cannot really solve any problems. The schmexpert's idea of management is to precipitate ersatz crises, so that he can use precooked solutions. Anyone who comes up with a different or better idea than his is condemned as "not understanding the problem."

The Egomaniac

The Egomaniac believes that the sun rises and sets on his royal arse. No one else in the company can do as good a job, so he delays decisions and "the real work" until he can get to it. The Egomaniac promotes and advances people on the basis of meeting his needs, not merit, so in a short time he is surrounded by junior egomaniacs willing to kiss the royal arse. He subscribes to *Fortune* for only one month's issue (*see* "Objectives").

The Wannabe

The Wannabe wants to be something he's not—a visionary, an engineer, a manager, or a hero. He isn't what he wants to be, but he doesn't want to hear this, so people around him have to pretend. Ironically, the Wannabe is usually very good at some role, but he is not content with it. Unfortunately, because he's the emperor, no one wants to tell him he's not wearing any clothes.

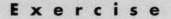

E x e r c i s e

Photocopy this section, circle the type of Boss Style that describes the person you work for, and leave it on his desk.

Objectives

Each year *Fortune* runs a story called "America's Toughest Bosses." In the 1993 version, the feature cited a contest run by Jim Miller, author of *The Corporate Coach*. Miller asked for the most gruesome description of a boss; the winner would receive a trip for two to Hawaii.

The boss of the winner of the contest had issued a memo to his staff that threatened termination for anyone who adjusted the office thermostat. He had also required employees to show a copy of the obituary if they took time off for a relative's funeral. Another contestant's boss had made his staff yelp like dogs to get their paychecks.* Obviously, some of these bosses are more stupid than tough.

Clearly, there are some serious nut cases to deal with, so driving your boss crazy is a formidable endeavor that can affect your career, your financial status, and your psyche. For this reason, do not start without first establishing your objectives.

Getting fired is probably not one of your objectives. Getting an even lousier boss is probably not one either. There are four acceptable objectives:

- Position yourself for the next boss (or become the next boss) when this one implodes. And he will implode.

- Make yourself attractive so that another, and one hopes, better, boss will hire you away.

- Provide yourself with a source of smug self-satisfaction because you're driving the jerk bonkers.

- Cause an improvement in your lousy boss. (Okay, so I was desperate for a fourth objective.)

Here are six tips and tricks to achieve these objectives—inspired in part by the definitive work on the subject of driving your boss crazy, *Crazy Bosses* by Stanley Bing.[1] You may not need all of them, but the more you use, the more likely you'll escape unscathed from a lousy boss.

*I'm not making this up. See "America's Toughest Bosses" by Brian Dumaine in *Fortune*, October 18, 1993, page 44.

▪ Pull Out the Needle

The most powerful weapon a lousy boss can use against you is fostering your dependence on him for approval and esteem. It's part of their game—if men are from Mars and women from Venus, then lousy bosses are from Uranus. Pull the needle out of your arm and consider him nothing more than another challenge at the office. You have the right to fulfill your needs, too.

▪ Deliver the Goods

Competence eclipses anything else you can do to drive your boss crazy. People who deliver the goods build a reputation, and reputation is power. By performing your job, you make yourself necessary to your lousy boss, and your lousy boss becomes unnecessary to you. By contrast, seeking revenge by not doing your job will inevitably hurt you.

▪ Build Bridges

While appearing loyal, build bridges with other parts of the organization. Sooner or later all lousy bosses get their due. When they do, you need to be prepared with a solid base of support above, below, and to the side of the boss you worked for. Pick some people and trust them. To go it alone is to invite isolation and despair.

▪ Fight for What's Right

Even the lousiest bosses—albeit deep down inside—know what's right. This includes knowing who should be promoted or given raises, the programs that should be implemented, and the services customers need. If you don't lower yourself to his capricious level and you fight for what's right, he'll at least know that you are competent, and most lousy bosses are cowards in the face of competence.

▪ Know More

A reputation is power, and so is knowledge. The halls of American business are filled with people who are indispensable to lousy bosses because they know more than the jerks they work for. Every boss wants to maintain or improve his position, and he can't do it without knowledge of how the company or marketplace works.

▪ CYA

When the sushi hits the fan, your lousy boss is going to look for people to blame. Knowing this, you must remember to cover your assets. When you work for a lousy boss, it's important to keep him informed, to make him prioritize your work, and, on a superficial level, make him responsible for what you have done. Finally, document your accomplishments to protect yourself.

Who's the Boss?

One last observation and one last story. First the observation: I've met many people who believe they worked too long for a lousy boss. I've never met anyone who believed he or she quit too early. *Capish?*

Now the story: In 1772 Prince Miklos Esterhazy promised the musicians of Franz Joseph Haydn's orchestra a vacation, only to renege several times. The musicians complained to Haydn, and he decided to communicate the situation to the prince with music.

Haydn composed the *Farewell Symphony* for this purpose. In the final movement of this piece, fewer and fewer musicians were needed as it progressed. As each musician finished his part, he would blow out a candle, and leave. Eventually the stage was empty. The prince figured out what was happening and gave the orchestra a vacation.

When you come right down to it, *everyone* is self-employed, and we are all responsible for our own happiness. So take control of your destiny, and if you can't work things out, blow out your candle and leave.

Interview: Charles Sampson

Charlie Sampson stands 5'4" tall and weighs 135 pounds. His competition stands about the same height at the shoulder but weighs approximately 1,500 pounds. Charlie's competition are bulls: he rides them at rodeos and he is so good at this that he has won the World Championship of Bull Riding.

An interview with a rodeo star may strike you as odd—or worse, irrelevant—in a business book. However, if you substitute the words "lousy boss" for "bull" in what follows, you'll see the value and relevance of Sampson's wisdom.

Q: What's the relationship between you and the bull?

We're out there competing against one another. He has a job to do; he knows that when he's in the bucket chute and the gate opens, the harder he bucks, the faster he turns, and the more power he throws at me, the more chance he'll get me off faster.

Q: A tame bull doesn't do you any good, right?

When he really bucks and really spins and really turns, that's the only way I'm going to be able to strut my stuff. We both have to be ready to perform. When he acts in seconds, I have to react in split seconds. He has to show his athletic ability because my performance is judged by how difficult he is to ride and how much control I have for eight seconds.

Q: What's going through your mind right before your ride?

When you're about to get on a bull, you're not really thinking about anything except that when the gate opens, you're going to be lifting on that rope, gritting your teeth, squeezing the bull, and reacting. You can get off to a bad start and recover, but normally if you get off to a bad start on a really tough bull, then you can't recover.

You want to make sure that everything is in your favor when you nod for the gate, and once you're ready, you nod for the gate, and just let it happen. I position my body for the first jump out of the chute. His momentum is going to try to rear me back, so I want to get out over the front end and ride his power. I'm also getting in sync with him for his next jump.

You're not trying to anticipate anything because you can over-anticipate. It's all up to the bull to pull you to where the next move is, and you just make your move. If you try to figure out a bull, you've already bucked yourself off. That's why I try to teach my students not to ask too many questions about what a bull's going to do.

Q: Is there a mental game going on between you and the bull?

The bull has a mind of his own because he's in the corral with other bulls,* and he's not really bumping shoulders with us, so we don't have a chance *per se* to stare each other down. The only time that he knows that I'm the person that's going to challenge him is when I start to put my equipment on his back.

I might push him around a little bit and see if he's awake and let him know, "Hey, it's me and you." He knows that somebody is irritating him, and I'm pumping myself up by telling him "I'm going to beat you today. I'm going to ride you. You're going to come out there and buck because that's the kind of animal you are. You're a great animal, but I'm letting you know that I don't care what you throw at me, I'm going to hang on."

Q: What is your relationship with the other riders?

They give you a little information on the bulls. Somebody might have had the bull in Oklahoma. Somebody might have had the bull in Texas. It might have gone out with two jumps and then gone to the left.

Q: Why would other riders help you when you're competing against them for prize money and standing?

Because that's the way it is in the rodeo circuit. You're only as good as the bull you have. You're not as good as the next man.

*Sounds like an executive staff meeting, doesn't it?

207

Q: Do you see any business lessons from your bull-riding career?

Some days the bull wants to buck, and some days he doesn't want to buck. One day you get jerked off the bull, and the next day you win the whole prize. All you want to do is approach your competitor with a positive attitude and be willing to get along.

See what I mean about the similarity of a bull and a lousy boss? Note, however, that there is an important difference between you and Sampson: he has enormous respect for his competition. The bottom line of Sampson's interview is:

- You and your lousy boss have jobs to do.

- You need each other.

- There's no sense in getting too mad until you can get off safely.

Note

[1]Stanley Bing, *Crazy Bosses: Spotting Them, Serving Them, Surviving Them* (New York: Pocket Books, 1992), 97–99.

Chapter 16

Preserve and Protect

The purpose of competition is not to beat someone down, but to bring out the best in every player.

Walter Wheeler

The Best Defense

D elighting customers is the best way to preserve and protect your company—that is, the best defense is a good offense. If you constantly please your customers, you can force your competition to react to you instead of playing their own game. For example, if you frequently introduce innovative new products, your competition may have to match you rather than fight in other areas such as service and support.

Anticipatory defense, preplanned as part of your offensive strategy, is the only kind of defense that has a role in driving your competition crazy. *Reactionary* defense—a response to your competition's offense—has no role unless you are a large company like Procter & Gamble. Then you can implement the three kinds of defensive tactics that we mere mortals only read about. The best source for information about these tactics is Michael Porter's *Competitive Advantage: Creating and Sustaining Superior Performance*.[1] Here is a brief summation of the techniques he describes:

- Raising structural barriers by acquiring companies, blocking distribution access, raising product-switching costs, raising the cost of product trials, and increasing capital requirements

- Increasing expected retaliation by communicating the willingness to respond, matching offensive efforts tit-for-tat, forming alliances with other organizations in preparation for a counterattack, accumulating and displaying a war chest, and preparing litigation

- Lowering the inducement for attack by reducing the profitability of the market and managing expectations for the outlook of the market

In the rare instances that you can erect these kinds of defenses, go for it, but for us mortals the Procter-&-Gamble-style defense doesn't work for three very good reasons:

- We can't get data fast enough to do anything with it. We may know how many widgets we sell every day (though I doubt most of us do), but we don't know how many are moving through the distribution pipe and into the hands of end users.

- Even if we could get data fast enough, we can't devise *and* implement defensive programs in time to take advantage of this information. We've got corporate hierarchies, sales forces, distributors, and dealers to work through. (So does Procter & Gamble, but it has clout—though nothing is a cinch.)

- Even if we could devise and implement defensive programs, these kinds of programs would distract us from the all-important goal of delighting customers. This is a nice way of asking, "Can we raise structural barriers?" The answer: Only in our dreams.

Defense for the Rest of Us

The closest many of us are ever going to get to Procter & Gamble is washing our clothes with Tide. This doesn't mean, however, that you can't implement a few defensive tactics of your own.

Ignoring Is Bliss

The first tactic is to put on a stoic and unemotional façade. Never, in the words of William Shakespeare, "protest too much." Don't lash out in anger. Don't inflame your competition by bashing it. Refusing to retaliate when your competition expects you to may irritate it more than anything else you can do.

Furthermore, retaliation may play into your competition's plans. According to legend, when Sinbad and his sailors landed on a tropical island, they saw coconuts high in the trees that would quench their thirst. They threw stones at the apes in the trees to irritate them. In retaliation, the apes grabbed coconuts and threw them at the sailors—playing right into their hands.

This is not to recommend burying your head in the sand and truly ignoring your competition. Though your external reaction is unemotional, your internal reaction can be furious action to create a new product or improve service. Again, remember that the ultimate defense is pleasing your customers, so don't act like an ape.

E x e r c i s e

Think of the times you've lashed out in anger—whether in business, sports, or relationships. Did your anger produce any positive results?

Nail a Negative to Your Competition

The second tactic is to attach a negative quality to your competition's company or product. Allen Kay alludes to this technique in his interview earlier: when Procter & Gamble tried to enter Wise's potato chip market in New York, he created an ad that made people associate the Procter & Gamble product with strange-sounding chemical ingredients.

Similarly, when F. W. Woolworth opened his first store, an existing merchant tried to fight him. This merchant hung out a sign that said DOING BUSINESS IN THIS SAME SPOT FOR OVER FIFTY YEARS. The next day Woolworth hung out a sign that said ESTABLISHED A WEEK AGO. NO OLD STOCK.[2]

Finally, according to marketing warfare mavens Al Ries and Jack Trout, Royal Doulton China positioned Lenox, its main U.S. competitor, as a lower-quality manufacturer through an ad whose headline said "Royal Doulton, the china of Stoke-on-Trent, England vs. Lenox, the china of Pomona, New Jersey." Clearly, Stoke-on-Trent, England, sounds like a more romantic place than Pomona, New Jersey for fine china to come from.[3]

The point of this defensive technique is to position your competition as illegitimate pretenders who do not have your best interests at heart—food additives, old merchandise, or lower-quality china.

Appear Unpredictable and Maniacal

The third tactic is to appear a little demented. Most organizations expect reasonable actions from their competition and prepare for them. Appearing like a maniac *kamikaze* often makes your competition hesitant to attack.

Virgin Atlantic Airways exemplifies this kind of company. It has offered free motorcycle or limousine rides to the airport, in-flight massages and manicures, personal video screens at each seat, and sleeper sections complete with sleepwear for business and first-class passengers. As mentioned earlier, Virgin accepted British Airways frequent-flyer miles in its program for free travel.

Richard Branson, the chairman of Virgin, is the pit bull of airline executives. For example, he has sued British Airways for unfair practices, libel, and antitrust violations. An avid balloonist, he claims to have offered to settle these legal claims with a trans-Atlantic balloon race against British Airways.[4]

At some point, when facing a company and entrepreneur like this, the competition figures doing battle just isn't worth the risk, and détente reigns. When this occurs, challenger and standard-bearer can coexist and both make reasonable amounts of profit.

Deliver Quick and Crushing Blows

The fourth tactic is to quickly retaliate. Your competition may view weakness as a signal to come in and help itself to your customers. The longer you tolerate an attack, the more costly it will be for you to defend yourself. A long-lasting price war, for example, may lower profitability for everyone.

Hindsight is 20/20, but General Motors could have delivered a quick and crushing blow to Honda when it first entered the U.S. market with its motorcycles. A few years later, General Motors also ignored Honda's more obvious action of introducing a car.

The goal is deterrence: stop the competition before it gets started and certainly before it gets entrenched. When delivering quick and crushing blows it is essential to determine whom to target. As a rule of thumb, look for small, young, and unknown companies, not big, obvious competitors. The young Turk is the one who usually gets you.

Prevent the Competition from Knowing You

Another way to thwart your enemy is to prevent it from learning about your company and business practices. If your competition is good, it's trying to learn as much about you as you're trying to learn about it. (If your competition is lousy, then you don't have to worry about it.) Here's what your competition is probably doing to you:

Misrepresentation

According to *How Competitors Learn Your Company's Secrets* from Washington Researchers Publishing, companies may use a variety of ruses that aren't flat-out lies but are designed to trip your employees into releasing confidential information.[5] Here are the common ones:

- No identity. A cheerful, friendly, and interesting interviewer can often get your employees to divulge information without their asking for identification.

- Job-position identity. This technique involves identifying oneself as "a market researcher in New York." This identity is true—all that's been omitted is that the market researcher works for your competitor.

- Smoke-screen identity. A company may have a competitive intelligence subsidiary. Or, a division employee may contact you and not mention that it is part of a parent company that you'd recognize as a competitor.

- Independent-research identity. Your competition may engage the services of a research company, and the research company may identify its name and position but not the client. Thus, a well-known industry analysis company may often call you for industry information, and then call your competitor.

Lying

The ruses mentioned above are on the borderline of being unethical. There's also the traditional method of lying. For example, your competitor or a person hired by your competitor may pose as a job applicant, a student doing a research project, a researcher doing an industry study, an employee of a trade or industry association pursuing company information, a competitor or agent claiming to be employed by your company, a government inspector or official, or a headhunter trying to fill an enticing position.

When you discover that your competition is playing this game, resist

---

E x e r c i s e

Call your company and use any of the ruses or lies to try to gain confidential information. How much do you get?

---

the adrenaline-induced urge to do unto them as they've done unto you. Here are three reasons why:

- It's illegal and unethical. The upside of what you might learn does not equal the downside of the wrath of the legal system.

- It communicates lousy values to your employees. Condoning lying starts your organization down a slippery slope that's very hard to climb back up.

- You're biting the karmic weenie. Even if you get away with it, the universe is keeping score, and the score always gets settled.

Seize the Leaks

On the other hand, don't lay down and scratch your tummy while your competition sends probes down your throat. Instead, *carpe lapsus!* (Roughly translated, seize the leaks!)

The first one is your mailing list. It amazes me that more companies don't filter their mailing lists. Three factors explain this:

- Some companies are too stupid to know that their competition is on their mailing list.

- Some companies are too lazy to filter their mailing lists. Perhaps they're busy explaining the latest "rightsizing" announcement.

- Some companies assume a world of "perfect information" in which sales, marketing, and press materials will get to the competition anyway, so they don't bother filtering the mailing list.

There's no excuse for stupidity and laziness. The more serious problem is the perfect-information misconception: "Our competition is so on top of things that it knows everything we've made public, so we might as well send information directly to them."

Nothing could be farther from the truth. Employees are busy people—even employees whose job it is to analyze the competition. If you don't stupidly send them information, they might not get it at all. Or, they might get it when it's too late to do anything about it.

E x e r c i s e

Examine your mailing list. If you see any of your competitors on it, are you stupid or lazy?

Now that we've reduced the leaks in your sales, marketing, and public relations departments, let's move on to employees. How do you prevent your employees from being duped into helping a competitor? According to Washington Researchers Publishing, your employees should observe this rule:

> Never reveal information to anyone that you would not reveal directly to your competitor.

Washington Researchers also recommends a four-step training process for employees:

1. Show your employees how leaking information is a detriment to your company and, therefore, to their own income and job security.
2. Teach your employees defensive techniques so that they can prevent the inadvertent release of information. Make your employees aware of the ruses that the competition is likely to attempt. Conduct role-playing exercises.
3. Create a positive work environment that fosters loyalty to your company. Most leaks are unintentional, but a disgruntled employee can purposely wreak extensive damage.

216

4. Establish and make your employees aware of your company's security procedures. Train your employees to refer intrusive questions to the proper people.

Though this chapter ends with defensive measures, remember that the ultimate way to drive your competition crazy is to delight your customer and avoid confrontation. To reinforce the gentle art of avoiding confrontation, the last interview is with an aikido instructor.

E x e r c i s e

At the next trade show, go to the booths of your competition and find an engineer, designer, or technical type. (They're easy to spot because they look like strangers in a strange land.)

Start by asking them a few hard-core technical questions about their product. See if this doesn't unleash a flood of confidential information that you'd never get out of executives.

Later, when you come back down to earth, ask yourself what would happen if your competition did the same thing to you.

Interview: Harry Eto

Harry Eto is eighty-eight years old, weighs 120 pounds, and stands 5'3". He is also a seventh-dan aikido instructor. (A ranking this high is as rare as a *Fortune* 500 executive with vision.)

Aikido is a Japanese martial art that exploits an opponent's motion, strength, and weight with various holds and circular movements. It stands in marked contrast to other martial arts that involve blocking blows and retaliating with kicks and punches.

Eto was one of the first students in America to study under Tohei Koichi, the creator of the particular style of aikido that Eto practices.

217

Until he was seventy-three years old, Eto worked in the construction industry. Now he concentrates on teaching aikido.

In this interview he discusses noncompetition—making the point that the best way to compete is to not compete. Eto believes it's better to control your *ki* than fight. In a nutshell, *ki* is the life energy that keeps the universe moving. Everyone possesses *ki*. Some people are simply better at harnessing it by making their mind, body, and spirit congruent.

Q: How do you contrast the physical and mental aspects of aikido?

Physically, I'm nothing [that is, because of his age and size]. In the early days, it was hard for me—all physical, not *ki*. The strong guy can beat you. The *ki* philosophy is very good: non-fighting, relax, don't worry. Be your own self. It's the hardest thing to do.

Many people just want to learn techniques and throw. Once you learn that your mind controls your body, then you can control your opponent's mind. We don't throw. We don't fight. We come from deep concentration of mental strength—not physical.

Every martial arts book recommends "mind training," but people don't practice that. They want to throw, but without the *ki*, you cannot throw. If you have a negative feeling, your mind won't work. No matter how strong you are, you cannot do your art correctly. Never mind the size of your opponent.

Q: Is aikido a fighting art?

We have no "opponents." Aikido is not a fighting art. Before we didn't practice *ki*, and we like to throw, but Shin Shin Toitsu aikido [the particular type taught by Eto] changed that. We don't throw. We don't fight. We have no pulling and pushing. We lead. We always move in circles.

There are five principles to lead a person. Number one: my *ki* must be extended—I can't be sleeping—I must know *what* you're doing. Number two: I have to understand *how* you're holding me. Number three: I have to respect your strength. Number four: I'm going to try to be in your place—not "fight" you. Number five: I'm going to lead with confidence.

218

I'm going to move your mind. My training is to bring your power into here [points to his abdomen].

Q: Have you ever used aikido in a fight?

No, I would be a loser if I used it because I'd be sued. The *ki* power is terrific. The guy would get a broken neck.*

Q: Did you use your *ki* training as a supervisor on the construction job site?

During the Depression and the war, I had a lot of boys working under me. We had to produce because if we didn't produce, we would have gotten fired. I didn't want the men to loaf. I "made" them work.

This was before I took aikido, and that was no way to run a gang. Every time they would see me coming, they were scared. They weren't going to produce because they were nervous. I was the loser.

I took a Dale Carnegie course in 1976. That's how I learned how to get along with people and how to influence people. From then on I took aikido at the same time. That improved my working ability. I could produce more. I could control the boys.

When they made a mistake, I didn't raise hell. We were taught: if you make a mistake, don't worry about it. It's done already. If you worry, it gets worse, so let's see the easiest way to correct the mistake.

Q: Do you have advice for businesspeople?

There's no need to strain. Come to play. Don't be tight. Smile. If you know your competition is wrong, and you tell him he's wrong, then you're fighting. Just go along. If he tries to hit you and you try to block, he's going to bring you down if he's stronger. If he hits, go the same way—go together—and then bring him around.

If you know your method is better, keep it here [gestures to his abdomen]. As long as you have it here, no one can take it away from

*During parts of our interview he demonstrated several aikido techniques to me. I assure you, he's not kidding about what he could do.

you. If you put it here [points to his head], you're going to be crazy and then you're going to be fighting.

Q: What if a person wanted to attack the competition?

Don't attack. Sit down. Be natural. Be yourself. Be humble. That way your mind is set already—the body is immovable. And you have to use this in your daily life—not just in the dojo [practice hall].

Notes

[1] Michael Porter, *Competitive Advantage* (New York: The Free Press, 1985), 487–500.

[2] Peter Hay, *The Book of Business Anecdotes* (Avenel, N.J.: Wings Books, 1988), 275.

[3] Al Ries and Jack Trout, *The 22 Immutable Laws of Marketing* (New York: HarperBusiness, 1993), 54.

[4] Jim Glab, "Virgin's Lost Innocence," *Frequent Flyer*, February 1994, 9.

[5] Leila Kight et al., *How Competitors Learn Your Company's Secrets* (Washington, D.C.: Washington Researchers Publishing, 1990), 35–42.

A Word Before You Go

The unexamined life is not worth living.

Socrates, from Plato's *The Apology* (trans. Benjamin Jorvett)

The Way of the Competitor

Competition provides a way to measure our capabilities and performance. At its best, it offers us a way to rise above our earthly limits and surpass ourselves. At its worst, competition can mutate into obsession, and obsession leads inevitably to tragedy.

A paradox quickly arises: to compete well, you must play to win, but playing to win can turn into an obsession, which deteriorates your ability to play to win. The way of a true competitor is to play *as if everything depends on the outcome and then walk away as if nothing depends on the result.*

As you play to win and try to drive your competition crazy, therefore, you need to constantly review your actions and check your motives. These are danger signs:

- You are willing to lie, cheat, steal, or break laws in order to defeat your competition.

- You delight in the calamities, legal investigations, and acts of God that wreak havoc on your competition.

- You no longer derive satisfaction from a job well done, and you prefer harming your competition to pleasing your customer.

- You cannot bring yourself to acknowledge what your competition has done well.

- You refuse to enter new markets or businesses because you fear defeat more than you relish success.

If and when you find yourself agreeing with these statements, it's time to reexamine what you're doing. It's likely that you are damaging your image in the marketplace, not making progress.

Rules of Thumb

T he concept of driving your competition crazy can turn unethical if doing in enemies, instead of pleasing customers, becomes your goal. To prevent this from happening, use these five rules of thumb to guide your efforts to drive your competition crazy:

- **Obey the law or your sense of ethics, whichever is stricter.** Obeying the law is often not good enough. Lying about delivery to prevent losing a customer, for example, is not a crime, but it is unethical. Your personal ethics may condone price fixing, but the law does not. If in doubt, always go with the stricter standard.

■ **Think as a member of society, not only as an employee of your company.** If you only think as an employee or entrepreneur, you'll probably concentrate on the welfare of the organization. However, we live in a vast, interconnected, and ongoing world. The pollution you cause, for example, to improve profitability will affect others—including your children and grandchildren.

■ **Put yourself in the shoes of your competition.** The Golden Rule works, so keep it in mind, especially when you are drawing outside the lines or seizing the day. This doesn't mean you have to be a wimp. There's a difference between outfoxing, outhustling, or outfighting, and cheating, stealing, or defrauding people.

■ **Read *Everyday Ethics* by Joshua Halberstam (Penguin Books, 1993).** This book is the finest book I've read about ethics for the real world. Here's a quote to illustrate what I mean: "The proper response to a lightweight is indifference, not hatred. Make your enemy work for you, not eat away at you."[1]

■ **If all else fails, double-check with your significant other.** If your spouse (I think that men are lucky because women make better consciences than men) doesn't think your idea is okay, it's probably not. Frankly, the fact that you have to ask your spouse usually means you shouldn't do what you're contemplating.

Play to Win

A few paragraphs ago I used the phrase "playing to win" as if its meaning was self-evident. It isn't. Playing to win means, borrowing a tennis analogy, that you hit the ball in the way that is hardest for your opponent to return it.

This doesn't mean that you should blister every shot at your competition—in some cases a lob or a dink is the hardest shot to return. In business, playing to win means running your business to make it as hard as possible for your competitor to steal your customers or attract new ones.

In business, playing to win is the finest thing you can do. It enables you to fulfill your potential. It enables your customers to improve their

---

Exercise

While writing this book, I read the transcript of Diane Sawyer's interview with Akio Morita, the CEO of Sony, on *60 Minutes* (January 8, 1989).

In the interview Morita confirmed that the first shirt-pocket-sized radios Sony built wouldn't fit inside a standard shirt pocket. In response, Sony ordered custom-made shirts with larger pockets for its salespeople. I thought this was a terrific example of how to drive your competition crazy.

My wife, however, told me not to include the story because Sony's action was a deceptive practice that misled the public unless the first models were prototypes and the first *shipping* models would fit in a normal shirt pocket. I could not verify this and doubted that it was true, so I cut the story.

Do you agree with her logic?*

---

lives and, conveniently, develop high expectations for all the companies they deal with. It enables your competition to operate at its highest level.

And what if you lose? Just make sure you lose while trying something grand. Avinash Dixit, an economics professor at Princeton, and Barry Nalebuff, an economics and management professor at the Yale School of Organization and Management, say it this way:

> If you are going to fail, you might as well fail at a difficult task. Failure causes others to downgrade their expectations of you in the future. The seriousness of this problem depends on what you attempt.[2]

---

*And isn't this a sly way of getting this example in the book anyway?

And Win to Play

I n its purest form, winning becomes a means, not an end, to improve yourself and your competition. In order to improve the world, companies have a moral obligation to play to win and force everyone to play at their highest level.

Winning is also a means to play again. The unexamined life may not be worth living, but the unlived life is not worth examining. The rewards of winning—money, power, satisfaction, and self-confidence—should not be squandered.

Finally, in addition to playing to win, you have a second, more important obligation: to compete again to the depth and breadth and height that your soul can reach.* Ultimately, your greatest competition is yourself.

Notes

[1]Joshua Halberstam, *Everyday Ethics—Inspired Solutions to Real-Life Dilemmas* (New York: Penguin Books, 1993), 21.

[2]Avinash Dixit and Barry Nalebuff, *Thinking Strategically—The Competitive Edge in Business, Politics, and Everyday Life* (New York: W. W. Norton & Company, 1991), 248.

*To paraphrase Elizabeth Barrett Browning.

List of Works Used

Immature artists imitate. Mature artists steal.

Lionel Trilling

Asprey, Robert. *War in the Shadows: The Guerrilla in History*. New York: William Morrow and Company, Inc., 1994.

Bennett, William, ed. *The Book of Virtues*. New York: Simon & Schuster, 1994.

Bing, Stanley. *Crazy Bosses: Spotting Them, Serving Them, Surviving Them*. New York: Pocket Books, 1992.

Boorstin, Daniel. *Cleopatra's Nose: Essays on the Unexpected*. New York: Random House, 1994.

Clancy, Kevin J., and Robert S. Shulman. *Marketing Myths That Are Killing*

Business: The Cure for Death Wish Marketing. New York: McGraw-Hill, Inc., 1994.

Czepiel, John. *Competitive Marketing Strategy*. Englewood Cliffs, N.J.: Prentice Hall, 1992.

D'Aveni, Richard. *Hypercompetition: Managing the Dynamics of Strategic Maneuvering*. New York: The Free Press, 1994.

Dixit, Avinash, and Barry Nalebuff. *Thinking Strategically—The Competitive Edge in Business, Politics, and Everyday Life*. New York: W. W. Norton & Company, 1991.

Drucker, Peter. *Adventures of a Bystander*. New York: Harper & Row, 1978.

Gardner, Martin. *More Perplexing Puzzles and Tantalizing Teasers*. New York: Dover Publications, Inc., 1969.

Gilad, Benjamin. *Business Blindspots*. Chicago: Probus Publishing Company, 1994.

Goldberg, Philip. *The Babinski Reflex*. Los Angeles: Jeremy P. Tarcher, Inc., 1990.

Gould, Stephen Jay. *Bully for Brontosaurus: Reflections in Natural History*. New York: W. W. Norton & Company, 1991.

Green, Michael, ed. *Illustrations for Biblical Teaching*. Grand Rapids, Mich.: Baker Book House, 1989.

Griffith, Joe. *Speaker's Library of Business Stories, Anecdotes, and Humor*. Englewood Cliffs, N.J.: Prentice Hall, 1990.

Halberstam, Joshua. *Everyday Ethics—Inspired Solutions to Real-Life Dilemmas*. New York: Penguin Books, 1993.

Hamel, Gary, and C. K. Prahalad. *Competing for the Future*. Boston: Harvard Business School Press, 1994.

Hay, Peter. *The Book of Business Anecdotes*. Avenel, N.J.: Wings Books, 1988.

Katz, Donald. *Just Do It: The Nike Spirit in the Corporate World*. New York: Random House, 1994.

Kingston, William. *The Political Economy of Innovation*. The Hague: Martinus Nijhoff, 1984.

Knight, Walter B. *Knight's Master Book of New Illustrations*. Grand Rapids, Mich.: William B. Eerdmans Publishing Company, 1956.

Lager, Fred. *Ben & Jerry's: The Inside Scoop*. New York: Crown Publishers, Inc., 1994.

LeBoeuf, Michael. *Fast Forward*. New York: G. P. Putnam, 1994.

Levinson, Jay. *Guerrilla Advertising: Cost-Effective Tactics for Small-Business Survival*. Boston: Houghton Mifflin Company, 1994.

Levinson, Jay, and Seth Godin. *The Guerrilla Marketing Handbook*. Boston: Houghton Mifflin Company, 1994.

McGartland, Grace. *Thunderbolt Thinking*. Austin, Tex.: Bernard-Davis, 1994.

Macrone, Michael. *Brush Up Your Bible!* New York: HarperCollins, 1993.

——. *Brush Up Your Shakespeare!* New York: Harper & Row, 1990.

Magrath, Allan. *The 6 Imperatives of Marketing*. New York: American Management Association, 1992.

Medawar, P. B. *Advice to a Young Scientist*. New York: Basic Books, 1979.

Melville, Herman. *Moby-Dick*. New York: Penguin, 1992.

Michalko, Michael. *Thinkertoys*. Berkeley: Ten Speed Press, 1991.

Mingo, Jack. *How the Cadillac Got Its Fins*. New York: HarperCollins, 1994.

Nagle, Thomas, and Reed Holden. *The Strategy and Tactics of Pricing*. 2d ed. Englewood Cliffs, N.J.: Prentice Hall, 1995.

Noble, Sarah, ed. *301 Great Management Ideas from America's Most Innovative Small Companies*. Boston: Inc. Publishing, 1991.

Oliver, Jack E. *The Incomplete Guide to the Art of Discovery*. New York: Columbia University Press, 1991.

Peters, Tom. *The Tom Peters Seminar*. New York: Vintage Books, 1994.

Porter, Michael. *Competitive Advantage*. New York: The Free Press, 1985.

Raphel, Murray. *Mind Your Own Business!* Atlantic City, N.J.: Raphel Publishing, 1989.

Rapp, Stan, and Thomas Collins. *Beyond MaxiMarketing: The New Power of Caring and Daring*. New York: McGraw-Hill, Inc., 1994.

Reid, Peter. *Well Made in America: Lessons from Harley-Davidson on Being the Best*. New York: McGraw-Hill, 1990.

Reynolds, Don, Jr. *How to Sharpen Your Competitive Edge*. Naperville, Ill.: Sourcebooks, Inc., 1994.

Richey, Terry. *The Marketer's Visual Tool Kit*. New York: American Management Association, 1994.

Ries, Al, and Jack Trout. *The 22 Immutable Laws of Marketing*. New York: HarperBusiness, 1993.

Rogers, David. *Waging Business Warfare*. New York: Kensington Publishing Corp., 1987.

Russo, J. Edward, and Paul J. H. Schoemaker. *Decision Traps: Ten Barriers to Brilliant Decision-Making and How to Overcome Them*. New York: Simon and Schuster, 1989.

Sakiya, Tetsuo. *Honda Motor: The Men, the Management, the Machines*. Tokyo: Kodansha International, 1982.

Schädlich, Gottfried. *Kriegslist gestern und heute (Tricks of War, Yesterday and Today)*, 2d ed. Herford/Bonn, 1979. As cited in Harro Von Senger, *The Book of Stratagems*. New York: Penguin, 1991.

Senge, Peter. *The First Discipline: The Art and Science of the Learning Organization*. New York: Doubleday Currency, 1990.

Shafritz, Jay. *Words on War*. New York: Prentice Hall, 1990.

Sherlock, Paul. *Rethinking Business to Business Marketing*. New York: The Free Press, 1991.

Shook, Robert. *Honda: An American Success Story*. New York: Prentice-Hall, 1989.

Slutsky, Jeff. *Streetfighting*. Englewood Cliffs, N.J.: Prentice-Hall, Inc., 1984.

Slutsky, Jeff, with Marc Slutsky. *StreetSmart Marketing*. New York: John Wiley & Sons, Inc., 1989.

Smith, Ken; Curtis Brimm; and Martin Gannon. *Dynamics of Competitive Strategy*. Newbury Park, Calif.: Sage Publications, Inc., 1992.

Solman, Paul, and Thomas Friedman. *Life and Death on the Corporate Battlefield*. New York: Simon and Schuster, 1982.

Stack, Jack. *The Great Game of Business*. New York: Doubleday Currency, 1992.

Tan, Paul Lee. *Encyclopedia of 7700 Illustrations*. Rockville, Md.: Assurance Publishers, 1979.

Tedlow, Richard. *New and Improved: The Story of Mass Marketing in America*. New York: Basic Books, 1990.

Trussell, Tait. *Beating the Competition: 150 Ways to Win New Customers for Your Small Business*. Lanham, Md.: Madison Books, 1993.

Ueland, Brenda. *If You Want to Write*. Saint Paul, Minn.: Graywolf Press, 1987.

Utterback, James M. *Mastering the Dynamics of Innovation*. Boston: Harvard Business School Press, 1994.

Vance, Sandra S., and Roy V. Scott. *Wal-Mart: A History of Sam Walton's Retail Phenomenon*. New York: Twayne Publishers, 1994.

Waldrop, M. Mitchell. *Complexity*. New York: Simon & Schuster, 1992.

Walton, Sam, and John Huey. *Made in America: My Story*. New York: Bantam Books, 1992.

Warriner, William. *101 Corporate Haiku*. Reading, Mass.: Addison-Wesley, 1994.

Winninger, Thomas. *Price Wars: How to Win the Battle for Your Customer*. Edina, Minn.: St. Thomas Press, 1994.

Index

At present, indexes cannot be electronically made, for the decisions required are of a far higher order than computers are yet capable of.

The Chicago Manual of Style, 14th edition

231

**Outside my window,
just one week each year, lilacs
are the bottom line.**

William Warriner